OSPREY
PUBLISHING

Union Monitor 1861–65

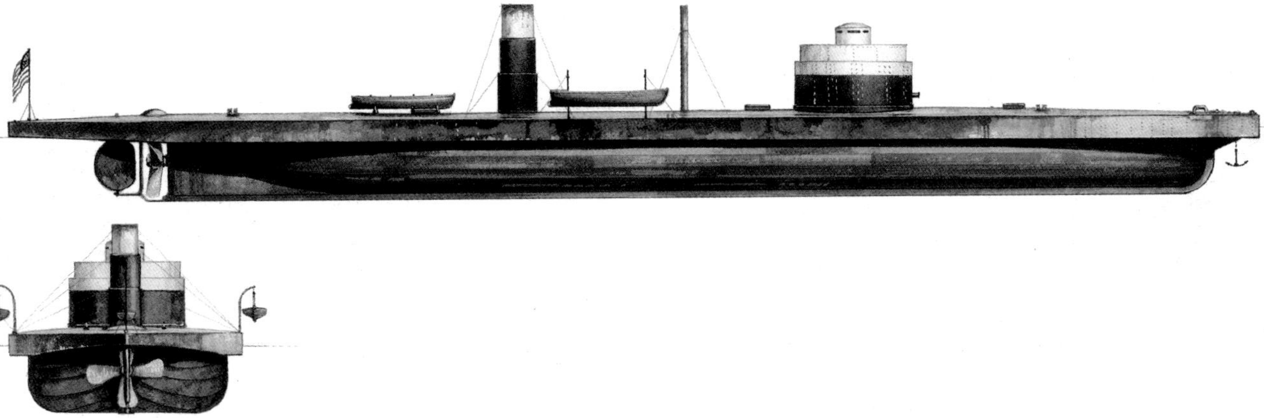

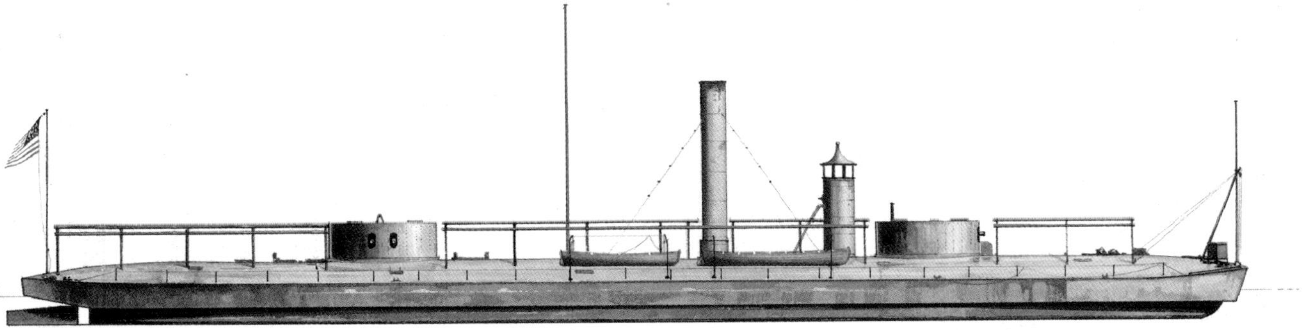

Angus Konstam · Illustrated by Tony Bryan

First published in Great Britain in 2002 by Osprey Publishing, Elms Court,
Chapel Way, Botley, Oxford OX2 9LP, United Kingdom.
Email: info@ospreypublishing.com

ISBN 1 84176 306 3

Editor: Marcus Cowper
Index by Alan Rutter
Design: Ken Vail Graphic Design, Cambridge, UK
Origination by Magnet Harlequin, Uxbridge, UK
Printed in China through World Print Ltd.

02 03 04 05 06   10 9 8 7 6 5 4 3 2 1

For a catalog of all books published by Osprey Military and Aviation
please contact:

The Marketing Manager, Osprey Direct UK, PO Box 140,
Wellingborough, Northants, NN8 4ZA, United Kingdom.
Tel. +44 (0)1933 443863, Fax +44 (0)1933 443849.
Email: info@ospreydirect.co.uk

The Marketing Manager, Osprey Direct USA,
c/o Motorbooks International, PO Box 1,
Osceola, WI 54020-0001, USA.
Email: info@ospreydirectusa.com

www.ospreypublishing.com

Artist's note

Readers may care to note that the original paintings from which the colour
plates in this book were prepared are available for private sale. All reproduction
copyright whatsoever is retained by the Publishers. All enquiries should be
addressed to:

Tony Bryan, 4a Forest View Drive, Wimborne, Dorset, BH21 7NZ

The Publishers regret that they can enter into no correspondence upon
this matter.

Key for Captions

USN: US Naval Historical Center, Washington, DC
HCA: Clyde Hensley Collection, Ashville, NC
Naval Institute: US Naval Institute, Annaolis, MD

UNION MONITOR 1861-65

INTRODUCTION

The popularity of the Civil War as a period of historic interest is reflected in the thousands of books on the subject, but of these, very few cover any aspect of the naval war. Even more noticeably, the ships of the Union Navy have been dealt with in a cursory fashion, as the focus of naval historical research has concentrated on the engagements themselves. It is hoped that this book will go some way towards making information on these vessels more accessible.

Even more so than her adversary the *Merrimac* (renamed the CSS *Virginia*), the USS *Monitor* represented a revolution in warship design. Not only was the vessel fully armored, but she mounted her guns in a revolving turret, which in theory was capable of firing in any direction. Following the first fight between two ironclads at the Battle of Hampton Roads (March 9, 1862) the North was swept by "monitor fever," as everyone from President Lincoln down became convinced that victory in the naval war would be achieved through the creation of a fleet of "monitor" ironclads. The original USS *Monitor* therefore spawned a host of successors, and gave her name to a new type of warship.

The USS *Monitor* as depicted in a Northern newspaper in 1862. Her diminutive and unusual appearance led the Confederates to underestimate her potential as a warship. (HCA)

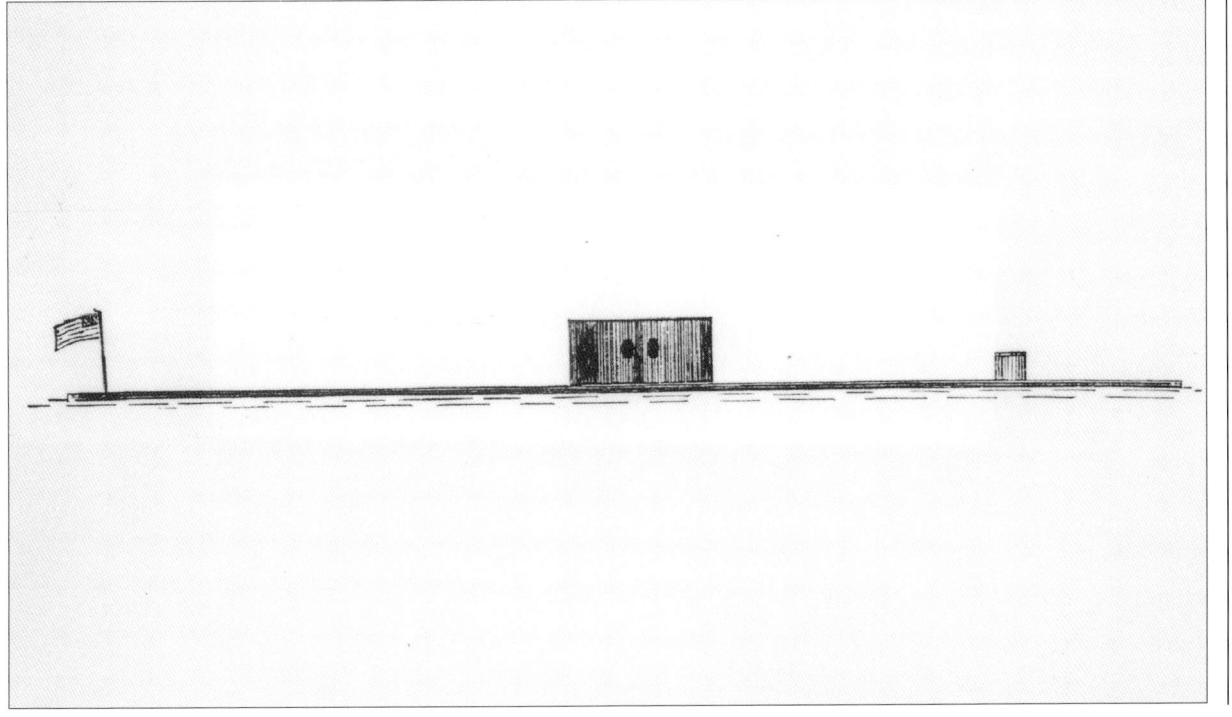

MONITOR DESIGN

Gideon Welles and the Navy Department

On March 4, 1861, Gideon Welles became President Lincoln's Secretary of the Navy. A month later the country was irrevocably plunged into war. When Lincoln approved the "Anaconda Plan," devised by General Winfield Scott, he committed his navy to a course for which it was ill-prepared. The strategy envisaged the encirclement of the Confederacy by both a naval blockade of Southern ports and a drive down the Mississippi River. Scott's Anaconda would constrict his victim, squeezing the life out the Confederacy by applying pressure to its borders. When the war was declared in April 1861 the US Navy had just over 90 warships at its disposal, but 48 were either in refit or were unfit for service, and another 28 vessels were deployed overseas. The remaining vessels were clearly insufficient to put into effect any blockade of the Confederate coast, so Welles instituted a huge expansion of the fleet. This included the acquisition and conversion of merchant ships until new purpose-built vessels could be constructed. He also considered the construction of armored warships. Both Welles and his Confederate counterpart were aware of the introduction of ironclad warships into the French and British fleets. During 1861 Welles became increasingly convinced that his naval plans would necessarily involve the adoption of a new breed of ironclad warships.

Welles had a limited knowledge of naval matters, but he was able to fill the Navy Department with highly competent subordinates. In August 1861 he made Gustavus V. Fox his Assistant Secretary, charging him with running the daily affairs of the department. His small department was gradually expanded to encompass the growing needs of the service. Originally it was divided into five Bureaus, overseeing construction, provisioning, medicine, dockyards and ordnance. A sixth Bureau of Steam Engineering was added later. For guidance on strategic matters, Welles formed a body referred to as the Blockade Strategic Board, while

This engraving was based on the photograph taken of the USS *Monitor* after her battle with the CSS *Virginia*, but depicts her without the subsequent modifications to her smokestacks, turret or pilothouse. (HCA)

another group advised him on scientific issues. An administrative section headed by a Chief Clerk covered more mundane matters and oversaw the navy's finances. Both the Senate and House of Representatives maintained standing Naval Affairs Committees, who occasionally met to investigate naval matters when required, and had the power to curb department spending.

Welles appointed businessman George D. Morgan to help the navy purchase and convert civilian ships, while another office in New York supervised dealings between the department and civilian contractors. This office, headed by Admiral Francis Gregory, inevitably became dubbed "The Monitor Board." The board operated independently of the department's own Bureau of Construction, headed by John Lenthall, a division of responsibilities that would cause problems in the future.

An even more influential advisory committee was formed in August 1861 after the Union authorities heard of Confederate plans to convert the former steam frigate *Merrimac* into an ironclad. This time Welles formed a three-man "Ironclad Board," whose members were to advise him on the development of ironclads, although none of them was expert in naval construction or ordnance. For all their lack of experience, it was this board which would recommend the construction of both the *Monitor* and the *New Ironsides*.

The naval yards were not equipped to build ironclad warships, so it was inevitable that almost all ironclads would be built under contract by private shipyards. Government policy also dictated that contracts were awarded to the lowest tender. A handful of private firms had the equipment and expertise necessary, and the majority of these were in New York or on the New Jersey shore. In many instances, contracts were awarded for the ship, while another more specialized firm was contracted to produce the engines. In other instances, the private contractor sub-contracted much of the work to improve profits.

The monitor USS *Chickasaw* and the former ironclad USS *Galena* depicted during the Battle of Mobile Bay (August 1864). This Milwaukee class warship commanded by Lieutenant-Commander George H. Perkins was one of four monitors to participate in the battle. (HCA)

The high cost of converting the necessary machinery and the rigorous government regulations surrounding contracts meant that only a handful of companies were willing to work on the construction of monitors, so a handful of yards specialized in the production of that type of vessel. One bizarre example of government regulations was the "Performance Bond," where the designer was liable for all costs until the vessel proved itself in naval service. This meant that when the USS *Monitor* fought the CSS *Virginia*, she was still legally owned by designer John Ericsson.

Somehow, despite such obstacles, the navy overcame the resistance of serving officers and the inertia of government bureaucracy to develop a fleet of ironclad warships. In the end Welles and his subordinates managed to find the right advisers, designers and private contractors to push forward the construction of an ironclad fleet. While the Confederate ironclad fleet was built as a result of a series of decrees by the government, the Union monitor fleet came about as a result of committees and entrepreneurial initiative. These naval and civilian advisers, these public servants and these designers, engineers and investors would combine to change the course of history.

Captain John Ericsson, the Swedish-born inventor of the USS *Monitor*. Under his direction dozens of monitors were built for the Union Navy during the war. (HCA)

The first ironclad contracts

Prior to the Civil War, the US Navy had made one unsuccessful attempt at producing its own ironclad. In 1842 the designer Robert L. Stevens was authorized to construct a large ironclad, although work was delayed until 1854. Stevens died two years later, and "Stevens' Battery" languished in his family's yard at Hoboken, New Jersey, until the outbreak of the war. Although the designer's brother offered to complete the work at his own expense in 1861, the navy viewed the vessel as a white elephant and rejected the offer. No more work was carried out on the battery until after the war.

When reports reached Washington that the Confederates were converting the former screw frigate *Merrimac* into an ironclad, Congress was duly alarmed, as the Union had no vessel with which to counter the Confederate warship. In response Welles asked Connecticut financier Cornelius S. Bushnell to use his influence with Congress to allocate funds to produce a Union ironclad squadron. Bushnell pushed a bill through both houses, and Welles formed his

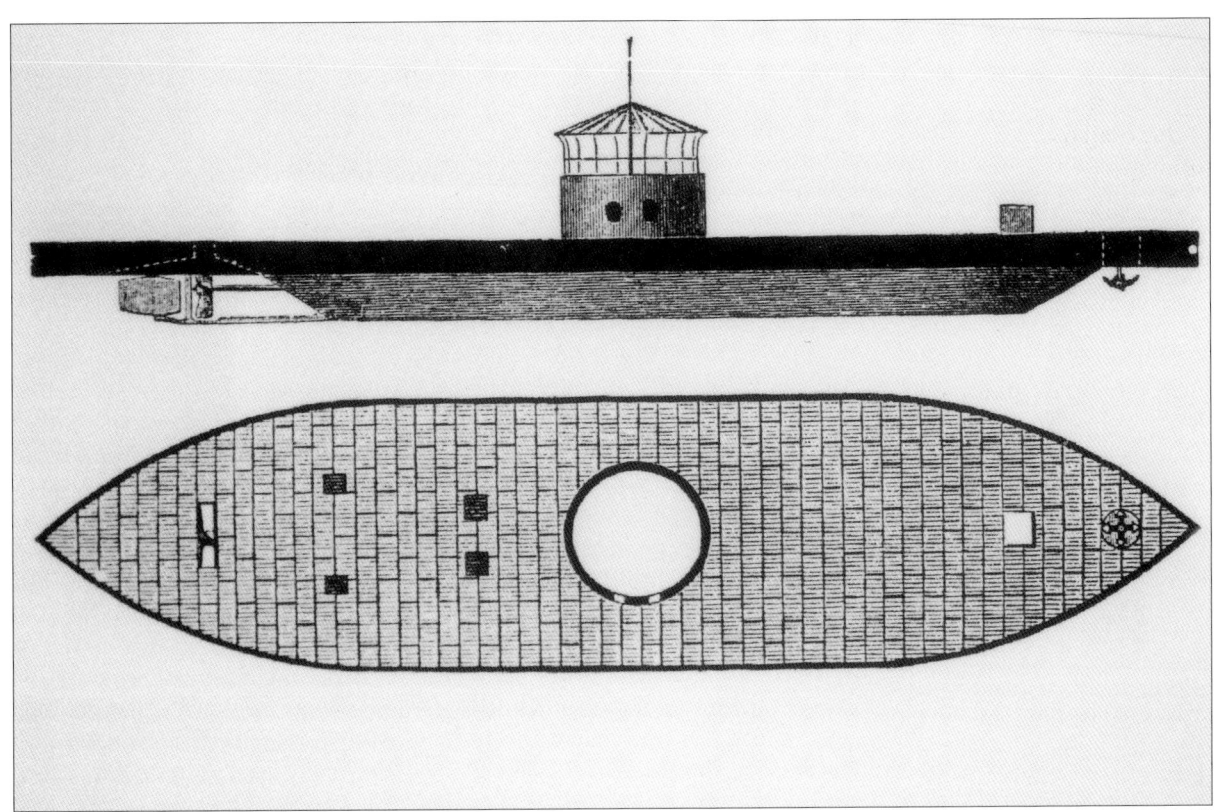

The side elevation and deck plan of the USS *Monitor*, shown with a protective awning rigged over her turret. This is how she would have appeared immediately after the Battle of Hampton Roads.

Ironclad Board on August 3, 1861, the day Congress allocated $1.5 million to be spent on new ironclad projects.

Welles's first step was to advertise for bids for ships "either of iron, or wood and iron combined, for sea or river service." He also specified the required draft, armor and coal capacity. Seventeen proposals were laid before the board, and on September 16, it presented its selection of three prototype vessels. The broadside ironclad (*New Ironsides*) proposed by Merrick and Sons of Philadelphia was almost a direct copy of the French *Gloire*, and the conventional design must have appealed to the board's more conservative members. A second successful bid was the ironclad gunboat (*Galena*), designed by Samuel Pook of Connecticut, who planned to have the vessel built at Mystic River, Connecticut. Both these vessels were named shortly before they were completed.

Bushnell influenced the award of the Connecticut contract, but in the process of lobbying he met Cornelius Delamater, the owner of a New York ironworks. The industrialist introduced Bushnell to his friend John Ericsson, and together they examined the plans for the ironclad gunboat. Ericsson showed the financier his own plans for an ironclad, and Bushnell was impressed with the design. He became a convert, and convinced both Welles and his business partners (John Winslow and John Griswold) that Ericsson's ironclad was the ideal vessel to counter the threat of the *Merrimac*. Despite the adamant opposition of board member Commander Charles Davis, Welles and Bushnell forced the board to accept the Ericsson plan. A determining factor was speed of construction, as the other vessels would take longer to build. Ericsson was awarded the third contract, and the *Monitor* legend began.

The *Monitor* and "monitor fever"

The hesitation of the Ironclad Board to approve Ericsson's design was understandable, as it was a completely revolutionary one. One board member even tried to force Ericsson to add masts and sails to the design, but the inventor refused. The design centered around a revolving gun turret containing two smoothbore guns. The guns were protected by eight layers of 1 inch iron plate, bent into gentle curves to create the 20 foot diameter turret. The hull was constructed in two parts, the upper portion sitting on top of the conventionally shaped lower hull like a raft. This upper portion was protected by two $\frac{1}{2}$ inch plates laid over the deck beams, and 5 inches of side armor in five 1 inch strips, backed by 25 inches of oak. When the guns were fitted the freeboard was less than 18 inches, meaning her hull was almost impossible to hit if fired at by another warship. The thin deck armor did mean the warship was vulnerable to plunging fire from fortifications.

The hull was flat-bottomed, with a 35 degree slope atop the bilge. The screw was protected by a recess in the upper deck section, which meant the vessel had a draft of just 10 ft 6 in. The screw was powered by two "vibrating-lever" engines designed by Ericsson himself, which propelled the vessel at a top speed of 6 knots. Smaller engines powered a ventilation system and the turret rotation mechanism, which took 24 seconds to turn the turret through a complete circle. The mechanism was controlled by a clutch inside the gun turret itself. Ericsson's 120 ton turret was designed to house two 15 inch Dahlgren smoothbores, but when the time came to mount the guns, only 11 inch pieces were available, so these were fitted instead. The turret was designed to turn on a thick central spindle, but first the turret itself had to be raised up off the deck from its "stowed position." When not in use it rested on a brass ring set in the deck. Iron shutters could be lowered over the gunports when the guns were not in use.

When she was completed, the *Monitor* was 179 feet long, with a beam of 41.5 feet, and looked like no warship which had ever been seen before. She was constructed at the Continental Iron Works at Greenpoint, Brooklyn, and newspapermen who watched her construction dubbed the vessel "Ericsson's Folly." The designer built the vessel with the financial support of Bushnell and his partners, who also benefited from the sub-contracting of parts of the project to their own yards, or those of their friends. As the date of the launch approached, Gustavus Fox wrote to Ericsson asking him what he planned to call the ironclad. He replied that his ironclad: "will thus prove a severe monitor to those [Confederate] leaders. Downing Street will hardly view with indifference this last Yankee notion, this monitor ... On these and many similar grounds I propose to name the new battery *Monitor.*"

The arrival of the USS *Monitor* in Hampton Roads, during the evening of March 8, 1862, came too late to prevent the destruction of two Union warships at the hands of the CSS *Virginia*. In this engraving the monitor is dwarfed by the wooden steam warship USS *Minnesota*. (HCA)

The *Monitor* was launched on January 30, 1862, and commissioned into service less than a month later. Lieutenant John L. Worden was placed in command of her 48 man crew, and on March 4, he steamed south towards Hampton Roads and his historic engagement with the *Monitor*'s Confederate opponent. Arriving in Hampton Roads on March 8, Worden was too late to prevent the first sortie of the *Virginia* that day, which resulted in the loss of two Union warships and the grounding of two more. When the *Virginia* renewed her attack the following morning, the *Monitor* sailed to meet her. For almost four hours the two ironclads battered each other, but with little visible effect. Soon after noon the *Virginia* retired to Norfolk as her deep draft made her a liability in the falling tidal waters of the Roads. The *Monitor* had proved her effectiveness, and held the larger Confederate ironclad at bay.

Worden was wounded in the engagement, and as he was taken to Washington for treatment, Gustavus Fox came on board to congratulate the crew and dine with the officers. By the time Worden reached the capital, the action was being hailed as a victory, and both Welles and Lincoln basked in the reflected glory. Both men were also keenly aware that as Ericsson's *Monitor* had countered the threat posed by the *Virginia*, the possibility of further Confederate ironclads breaking the Union blockade was unlikely. The industrial North could easily out-produce the South. A whole fleet of monitors would effectively seal off the Confederacy from the rest of the world. Lincoln also realized that the Battle of Hampton Roads was the last genuine opportunity for the Confederates to encourage the political and naval intervention of Britain and France to break the blockade. The failure of the *Virginia* to defeat the *Monitor* sealed the long-term fate of the Confederacy.

After the Battle of Hampton Roads, as the two days of fighting became known, "monitor fever" swept the country. While the crewmen of the USS *Monitor* were lauded as heroes, Ericsson and his ironclad design were also placed on a pedestal. The only group who maintained some reservations about the monitor design were the officers of the ship and their Navy seniors. Although Ericsson later claimed his design was created exclusively to counter Confederate ironclads, this was after the debacle at Fort Sumter in 1863. In early 1862 he had written that: "this structure [the *Monitor*] will admonish the leaders of the Southern rebellion that the batteries on the banks of their rivers will no longer present barriers to the entrance of the Union forces." The views of the navy's leaders were swept aside in the general excitement, which even extended to include President Lincoln and Welles. Other ironclad designs were abandoned in favor of monitors, and Ericsson could do no wrong.

This longitudinal interior view of the USS *Monitor*'s rudder, engine and propeller shaft assembly shows the overhanging upper deck structure which protected the rudder and screw from damage. (HCA)

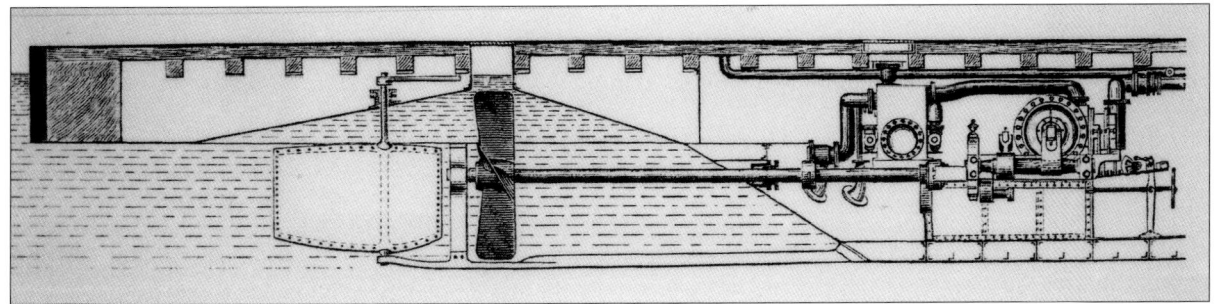

Casemate ironclads

The success of the *Monitor* effectively ensured that three other ironclad prototypes would not lead to further vessels of their type. The USS *New Ironsides*, the USS *Galena* and the USS *Keokuk* therefore represented a dead end in warship design. Of these, the *New Ironsides* was by far the most powerful. Displacing over 4,000 tons, she carried an armament of 16 guns, mounted in broadside batteries. Although fitted with a ram bow, she was too under-powered to use it in anger. The central casemate was protected by up to 4.5 inches of iron backed by 15 inches of wood, which made her impervious to most Confederate shot. During her attack on Fort Sumter in April 1863, sandbags were added to provide more protection to her deck. She served as Admiral Du Pont's flagship in this battle, and although an under-powered and awkward vessel, her formidable firepower and adequate protection ensured her position as one of the most valuable vessels in the fleet. She also had the distinction of being in action more times than any other Union warship in the blockading squadrons.

The USS *Galena* was built in Mystic, Connecticut, while her engines came from New York. She carried six guns, capable of firing from fixed broadside gunports on either side of her hull, but her 3.25 inch armor lacked extensive wooden backing, and her deck was unarmored. Her iron plating was fitted in the form of rows of interlocking iron planks, and although her tumblehome was designed to encourage shot to glance off, it also left her more vulnerable to plunging fire. It was unfortunate that her first action was against the Confederate fortifications at Drewry's Bluff on the James River (May 15, 1862), and the ironclad was badly damaged in the engagement. She was subsequently stripped of her armor and recommissioned as a wooden gunboat.

The former ironclad USS *Galena* was sketched after the Battle of Mobile Bay, following her conversion from an ironclad gunboat to a wooden one. She fell victim to monitor fever, and was relegated from the ranks of the ironclad fleet even though she could still have played a useful role. (HCA)

The USS *Keokuk* was an "armored gunboat" designed by Charles W. Whitney, a financial partner of John Ericsson, and her plans were first submitted to the Navy Department as early as April 1861. She had high, sloping sides and a cambered deck, topped by two small casemates which resembled gun turrets, but were immobile. Each was designed to house a single 11 inch Dahlgren on a 360 degree pivot mounting, capable of firing through one of three fixed gunports. An armored pilothouse was sited between the two casemates. Although Whitney's plans were dismissed, he re-submitted them in the wake of Hampton Roads, and was given a

contract. The *Keokuk* was duly built at the Underhill Yard in New York, and she was commissioned in March 1863, in time to participate in the attack on Fort Sumter. She proved a costly disaster, as her thin armor proved incapable of preventing the penetration of Confederate shot. After being hit over 90 times (including 14 hits below the waterline), her crew were unable to prevent her from taking in water, and she sank the following morning.

The USS *Galena* in the summer of 1862, viewed from forward of the funnel on the port side, looking astern. Her pronounced tumble-home and her steel hull cladding are clearly visible. (Naval Institute)

The casemate ironclad USS *New Ironsides* photographed soon after she was commissioned in August 1862. The shutters of her gunports have been opened to provide extra ventilation. Her bark-type sailing rig was later removed. (Smithsonian)

Passaic class

Within a week of Hampton Roads, Congress approved the allocation of funds for a new class of ten improved versions of the *Monitor*, following plans drawn up by Ericsson while the original *Monitor* was still under construction. These vessels were described as "monitors," the first use of the term as a type of vessel rather than an individual ship. These vessels became known as the Passaic class. Ericsson's design was almost rejected in favor of plans drawn up by John Lenthall, the Chief of the Bureau of Construction and Repair. Lenthall's ironclads relied on the superior British-designed Coles turret, and might well have become more effective warships, but extensive lobbying by Ericsson and his financial partners ensured he rather than Lenthall was awarded the contract, provoking a feud between the two men that would outlast the war.

The reports of the *Monitor*'s officers were examined by Ericsson and the Navy Department, and their suggestions were incorporated into the new design. All the monitors were 200 feet long, with a 46 foot beam, making them larger and more stable than the original *Monitor*, but they retained their prototype's shallow draft. Compared to the *Monitor* the hull was more streamlined, with a slight sheer towards the bow and stern, and a cambered upper deck to allow breaking waves to run off the hull more easily. The most significant post-Hampton modification was to mount the pilothouse on top of the turret, which allowed better communications between the conning position and the gun turret. The turret was designed to carry two 15 inch Dahlgren smoothbores, but a shortage of suitable ordnance forced the compromise of fitting one 15 inch piece alongside an 11 inch Dahlgren smoothbore. All these considered, the Passaic class monitors were a great improvement over their prototype.

The failings of the Passaic class reflected the inadequacies of the original *Monitor*. When they were conceived, these vessels were designed to fight enemy ironclads, not fortifications, so the deck armor remained thin. Similarly, Ericsson's engines were inadequate, and the Passaic class ships were barely able to steam at 6 knots. The vessels should have been equipped with improved engines, but Ericsson's vibrating-lever engines were fitted with only minor modifications. As the vessels were larger than the *Monitor*, it was inevitable that they would be under-powered.

The Passaic class monitor USS *Weehawken* in an engraving based on a photograph taken of the ironclad within days of the disastrous attack on Fort Sumter in April 1863. The monitor was hit 53 times during the battle. (HCA)

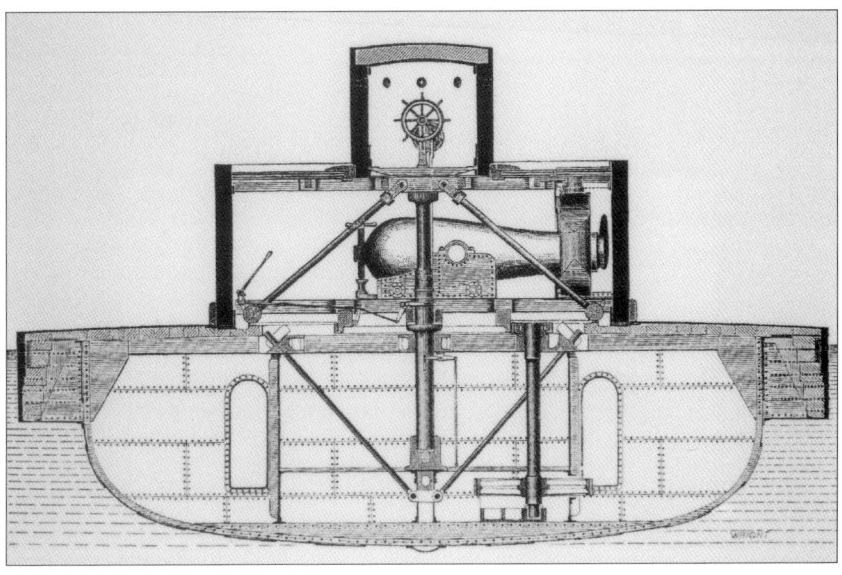

The USS *Montauk* commanded by John Worden (the former commander of the *Monitor*) attacked and destroyed the Confederate paddlewheel raider *Nashville* on the Ogeechee River in Georgia on February 28, 1863. Note how the monitor is shown towing her boats astern to reduce the risk of damage to them. (HCA)

Contracts for these vessels were placed in six different yards from Boston, Massachusetts, to Wilmington, Delaware, and the first of them, the USS *Passaic,* was commissioned in December 1862. By the time Admiral Du Pont launched his monitors against Fort Sumter in April 1863, eight more Passaic class monitors were available, and seven in all

This cross-section of a Passaic class monitor emphasizes the improvements of the design over the USS *Monitor*. The location of the pilothouse over the gun turret ensured better communication between the captain and the gunnery officer. The turret rotation mechanism was also far more efficient, allowing a faster rotation speed. (HCA)

A Passaic class monitor, possibly the USS *Lehigh*, photographed on the Stono River south of Charleston in late 1864. Her turret and pilothouse are screened by canvas awnings, and a small howitzer can be seen on her forecastle. (Naval Institute)

took part in the attack. A tenth Passaic class, the USS *Camanche,* was built in San Francisco, and commissioned in May 1865.

The attack on Fort Sumter in April 1863 was a failure, and most of the participating monitors were damaged by non-penetrating hits. The action also highlighted the vulnerability of the joint between the turret and the hull, as several monitors had their turrets jammed by shot damaging the brass turret ring. That summer a protective ring was added around the base of the turret, and extra plate was added to the exterior of the pilothouse. As the engagement between the USS *Weehawken* and the ironclad CSS *Atlanta* showed, these monitors were highly effective in combat against other ironclads, the task they were designed to perform. They were less well suited to attacking powerful fortifications.

Canonicus class

As Ericsson's star stood high in the firmament in 1862, the designer was virtually assured of further contracts, and in July he was awarded a contract to build nine more ironclads. The result was the Canonicus class, a further development of Ericsson's original *Monitor* design. Five of these were commissioned before the war ended. Ericsson had been working on improvements to his *Passaic* design as early as the summer of 1862, primarily to increase their speed and performance. Improved versions of his own engines were installed, and sharper bows and longer hulls improved their passage through the water. The ordnance supply problems which plagued the navy in 1862 had been overcome, so the turrets carried two 15 inch Dahlgren smooth-bores, with improved carriages to allow the muzzles to protrude further through the gun ports. The ships were laid down in the fall of 1862, five in yards on the Atlantic coast, and four more in yards in Pittsburg and Cincinnatti. Although the monitors built in the

The bombardment of Fort Fisher, North Carolina (January 13–15, 1865), lasted over 60 hours. In this lithograph three Canonicus class monitors (USS *Mahopac*, USS *Canonicus* and USS *Saugus*) accompanied by the USS *Monadnock* are shown in the background, bombarding the Confederate fort at close range. (HCA)

Atlantic yards were all commissioned in 1864, none of the vessels produced in western yards was ever commissioned.

These monitors were all still on the stocks when the reports of the performance of the Passaic class monitors at Charleston were read by Welles and the Navy Department. Consequently recommendations were made to incorporate modifications to the Canonicus design. The turret was to be protected by a thick glacis ring, and the pilothouse was to be heavily armored.

Three monitors of this class were commissioned in April 1864, and two more were added to the list by the fall. A further two vessels (*Catawba* and *Oneota*) were built in Cincinnati, Ohio, but were never commissioned. Instead, they were sold to the Peruvian government, which renamed them *Atahualpa* and *Manco Capa*. Two more vessels were laid up at New Orleans, and were never commissioned until the 1870s. The five Canonicus class monitors which saw service during the war proved effective warships, although the USS *Tecumseh* was sunk by a torpedo (mine) as she entered Mobile Bay. The modifications incorporated during construction also ensured they were better suited to engagements with fortifications than previous Ericsson designs.

The USS *Canonicus* photographed long after the war, at a naval review held in Hampton Roads in 1907. Although decommissioned in 1877, she remained in mothballs until the review, and was sold the following year. Remarkably, apart from her smokestack, her appearance had remained unchanged since the end of the war. (USN)

USS *Roanoke*

Described as the unfortunate victim of "monitor fever," the steam frigate USS *Roanoke* was commissioned in 1857, and she was present at the Battle of Hampton Roads in March 1862. As a result of the engagement, she was sacrificed on the altar of naval experimentation, and less than three weeks later she was decommissioned, and sent to the aptly named Novelty Iron Works in New York city. The conversion of the steam frigate was the brainchild of John Lenthall (Chief of Naval Construction) and Benjamin F. Isherwood (Chief of Steam Engineering). Her upperworks were cut down to her main gundeck, and it was planned to install four Coles turrets on her upper deck. As these were unavailable, Lenthall reluctantly agreed to substitute three Ericsson turrets instead. Each turret carried one smoothbore and one rifled gun. The hull was protected by 4.5 inches of iron in one-piece slabs rather than in the usual series of 1 inch laminated plates. *Roanoke* was recommissioned in

The ironclad ram USS *Roanoke* was converted from a steam frigate by cutting down her upper hull and removing her masts. Her four smoothbores and two rifled guns were mounted in three turrets, which made the vessel top-heavy, and strained the existing wooden frames of the hull. She was never used in action. (USN)

late June 1863, but on her voyage back to Hampton Roads it was discovered she was too top-heavy to operate safely in open waters. The wooden deck was also strained by the weight of the turrets. The design was considered a costly failure, and she remained as a harbor defense ship in Hampton Roads for the remainder of the war.

A similar wrong turning was the *Dundenberg*, a casemate ironclad which loosely resembled the CSS *Virginia*. Designed by James Lenthall, she was a 7,000 ton ironclad ram whose technical requirements and attendant problems strained the Brooklyn Navy Yard. Lenthall's original design incorporating two turrets was altered following the failure of the *Roanoke*, and the casemate was the alternative solution. The use of unseasoned timber caused delays in construction and, although she was launched in July 1865, she was never completed. The following year she was sold to France.

Milwaukee class

Although the study of Mississippi River ironclads is beyond the scope of this book, 24 ironclads were built, converted or captured and used on the Mississippi River and its tributaries during the war. Of these, nine were monitors. Unlike the rest, the four monitors of the Milwaukee class were not just pure riverine vessels, but were capable of operating in the coastal waters of the Gulf of Mexico.

In May 1862 the Navy Department awarded a contract to James Eads, a shipbuilder and designer who owned the Union Iron Works at Carondolet, Missouri, a few miles south of St Louis on the banks of the Mississippi. Eads had already successfully built ironclads to designs supplied by Samuel Pook. His new design was for a twin-turreted monitor, combining the shallow draft of most riverboats with a cambered armored deck with a low freeboard. His vessels were driven by four horizontally laid engines, which powered four screws, giving the monitors a top speed of 9 knots. The turret configuration was also unusual, as he designed the vessels to carry an Ericsson after turret and

a turret of his own design further forward. These Eads turrets were a significant improvement over the Ericsson design as they not only used steam engines to rotate the turret, but steam power was also used to run the guns in and out, elevate them and operate the gunport stoppers. Unlike the Ericsson turret which turned on a central spindle, the Eads turret extended below the upper deck and rotated on bearings running in a circular track. These ironclads were commissioned in the spring and summer of 1864, and served in the Western Gulf Blockading Squadron. Both the USS *Chickasaw* and the USS *Winnebago* participated in the Battle of Mobile Bay in 1864, where they proved their effectiveness in action against the ironclad CSS *Tennessee*. It has been argued that of all the monitors produced during the war, the Eads vessels were the most successful.

Twin-turreted monitors

The Navy Department had considered the creation of twin-turreted monitors since the spring of 1862, and in the frenzy of "monitor fever," four were ordered in 1862, while a further vessel was ordered the following year. Of these, only two were commissioned before the end of the war.

Shipbuilder and designer George W. Quintard was given a contract to produce a twin-turreted monitor on May 26, 1862, less than three

The Milwaukee class monitor USS *Chickasaw* shown engaging the ironclad CSS *Tennessee* during the closing stages of the Battle of Mobile Bay (August 1864). Although they were designed for use on the Mississippi River and its tributaries, two Milwaukee class monitors participated in the battle.

The powerful twin-turret monitors USS *Miantonomoh* (left) and the USS *Terror* (formerly the *Agamenticus*) photographed at anchor off Portland, Maine, in 1870. Although laid down in 1862, both were commissioned after the end of the conflict. (Peabody Museum, Salem, Massachusetts)

weeks after the Battle of Hampton Roads. His vessel was to be constructed entirely from iron, giving the hull a far greater strength and longevity. The *Onondaga* was built at the Continental Ironworks in Brooklyn (the same yard that built the original *Monitor*), while the engines were built at the neighboring Morgan Iron Works, which was owned by Quintard. Her armament was varied, with a 150-pdr Parrot rifle and a 15 inch Dahlgren smoothbore in each turret (the rifled guns were mounted on the left of each pair). The USS *Onondaga* was 226 ft long and almost 50 ft wide, making her shorter but more beamy than previous monitors. She entered service in March 1864, and served on the James River throughout the war. During the Battle of Trent's Reach (January 24, 1865) her 15 inch shot penetrated and seriously damaged the ironclad CSS *Virginia* (*II*), and prompted a Confederate retreat. Although she had her faults (namely her poor coal capacity and engines), she was regarded as a highly successful design.

By contrast the Monadnock class of two twin-turreted monitors (*Monadnock* and *Agamenticus*) were criticized for their poor hulls. The subsequent *Miantonomoh* and *Tonawanda* were both slight variations of the same design. All four vessels were designed by John Lenthall, and were seen from the outset as Navy Department vessels. Lenthall decided to use wood for their construction (as had Ericsson in his single-turreted monitors) because it permitted the vessels to be constructed in naval yards. Consequently, the *Monadnock* was built in the Boston Navy Yard, the *Agamenticus* in Portsmouth, the *Miantonomoh* in Brooklyn and the *Tonawanda* in the Philadelphia Yard. Lenthall replaced Ericsson's raft hull with a more streamlined design, and raised the freeboard, which increased the vessels' seakeeping qualities at the expense of protection. As the hulls carried 4.5 inches of iron backed by oak, this was not seen as a significant problem. The engines (designed by Benjamin Isherwood) were powerful, generating speeds of up to 9 knots. Lenthall's mistake was to rely on wooden frames to support the twin turrets. Like his *Roanoke* conversion, the weight of the turrets weakened the structural integrity of the vessels, and the hulls were prone to rotting and cracking. Only the USS *Monadnock* was in service before the end of the war. She participated in the attack on Fort Fisher in January 1865, and successfully sailed to San Francisco via Cape Horn soon after the end of the war.

Four additional twin-turreted ironclads (referred to as the Kalamazoo class) were commissioned in late 1863 and early 1864, based on a design submitted by Benjamin F. Delano. Like the Lenthall ironclads, these vessels were designed to be constructed in the same four naval yards, which lacked the facilities to construct metal-ribbed vessels. These were true white elephants, and their planned displacement of 5,660 tons was almost six times that of the original *Monitor*. Designed as ocean-going monitors, they were never completed, and rotted on the stocks.

The powerful twin-turret ironclad USS *Onondaga*, photographed on the James River during the summer of 1864. She participated in several actions on the river, including the Battle of Trent's Reach on January 24, 1865. (Naval Institute)

Ericsson's ocean-going monitors

The USS *Dictator* was another Ericsson design, a monitor which was almost twice the size of his original *Monitor*. This was Ericsson's vision of a "sea-going monitor." His original name for the vessel was *Protector*, but the Navy Department favored a more aggressive name. She differed from his previous designs in several vital aspects, apart from the sheer scale of the vessel. The overhang of the upper hull was less pronounced than in previous ironclads, and at the bow the upper and lower hull sections were blended together to form a unified bow structure. This meant she had cleaner hull lines than previous monitors, and therefore made it easier for her engines to drive her through the water. She also had twice the draft of a Passaic class monitor, which made her a better seagoing vessel, but reduced her operational value in coastal waters. The wide smokestack and a ventilation shaft were armored, while a light flying bridge (or "hurricane deck") was added behind the turret. Her two 15 inch Dahlgrens were protected by an impressive 15 inches of armor. The *Dictator* was commissioned in November 1864, but engine failure prevented her taking part in the bombardment of Fort Fisher, and she played no further part in the conflict. Nevertheless she remained in service for another two decades after the war, and she was generally regarded as a useful coastal defense vessel.

Her half-sister *Puritan* was laid down in 1863 in the Continental Yard in New York, and was virtually an enlarged version of the *Dictator*.

Ericsson planned to arm her with two of Dahlgren's new 20 inch smoothbores, but production problems prevented their delivery before the end of the war. Although the *Puritan* was launched in July 1864, she was never completed and she languished in New York for another decade before she was scrapped. Although impressive, these large sea-going ironclads went against the trend of concentrating on shallow draft coastal and riverine monitors. They were also extremely costly, and at $1.3 million, they were five times more expensive than the original *Monitor* and double the price of the USS *Canonicus*.

The light-draft monitor fiasco

The Navy Department decided that there was a need for shallow draft monitors which were capable of operating in extremely shallow rivers, such as the smaller tributaries of the Mississippi. Ericsson produced preliminary sketches for a design in two days during the summer of 1862, but went no further than to submit these to Gustavus Fox. Fox then passed the draft plans to Chief Engineer Alban B. Simers for study. Instead, Simers developed fully-fledged plans, then modified these following the attack on Fort Sumter in April 1863. Simers was attached to the Monitor Board in New York, and John Lenthall had little or no communication with it, while Ericsson and Simers fell out, and refused to co-operate on the project. The result was that the plans were approved without serious scrutiny, and Simers ordered the construction of 20 of his light draft monitors, and $14 million was appropriated for their construction. Dubbed the Casco class, the vessels were built in Atlantic yards and also in Pittsburg, Cincinnatti, and St Louis.

Of the 20 Casco class monitors ordered, only three entered service before the end of the war (*Casco*, *Chimo* and *Naubuc*). The design proved a disaster, as although the original design was reasonably sound, a stream of subsequent modifications made by Simers increased the weight of the vessels, but failed to compensate for the extra stress on the hull. The result was a series of vessels whose freeboard was less than 3 inches, and whose wooden frames were unable to support the weight of the reinforced turret structure. Simers was removed from control of the project, and Ericsson was called in to try to remedy the fiasco. The

When the war ended many of the monitors were mothballed. In this photo a turretless Casco class monitor lies in the foreground, while three Canonicus and Passaic class monitors are seen astern of her in the background. The turretless vessel has been tentatively identified as either the USS *Casco* or the USS *Chimo*. (USN)

The Casco class monitor USS *Chimo* (left) and the powerful USS *Tonawanda* (right) pictured at anchor off the Washington Navy Yard after the war. Although the *Chimo* was commissioned in January 1865, the *Tonawanda* was still being completed at the war's end. The captured Confederate raider *Stonewall* is visible in the background. (USN)

only practical solution was to raise the hulls of the monitors by almost two feet, which added to the weight of the vessels. Consequently, just before the first vessels were completed, the turrets were removed, and the first three monitors were converted into torpedo boats, armed with 11 inch Dahlgrens on an open mount, and a spar torpedo, placed on a retractable pole extending from the bows of the vessels. None saw active service, but they were used as guard boats. The remainder of the Casco class were laid up as they were completed, an embarrassing flotilla of white elephants. The entire fiasco was the result of a lack of control within the Navy Department, and Welles and his senior subordinates were duly castigated for the affair.

MONITOR CONSTRUCTION METHODS

At the start of the war, Naval Yards were not equipped to build ironclad warships. While facilities were gradually improved in these dockyards, this took time, and private iron foundries had to fill the gap. In fact, all but a handful of wartime monitors were built under contract with private yards, under the supervision of the Monitor Board in New York.

This cross-section of the USS *Monitor* is based on a series of more detailed plans and shows the forward facing of her two boilers and furnaces. A similar boiler configuration was adopted in Passaic and Canonicus class monitors. (HCA)

The original *Monitor* was designed to allow its construction using existing facilities in these foundries, and by conventional metal fabrication techniques. Ericsson also provided detailed plans of every aspect of construction, allowing the fabrication of different elements in other sites. This speeded production, and when the elements were

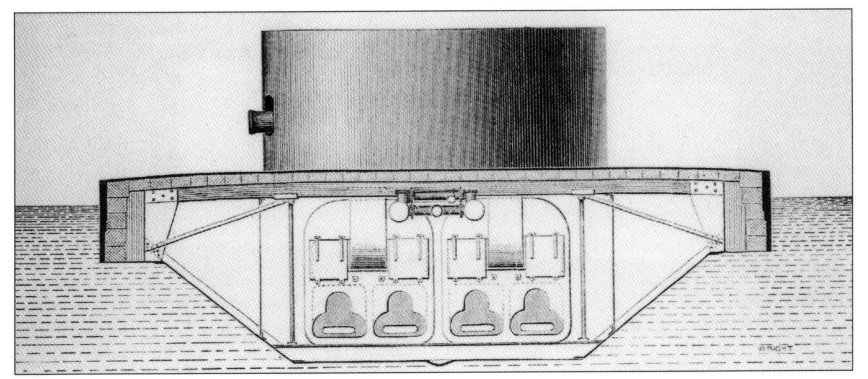

A planing machine like this was used to produce a smooth finished surface to the armored plates used to protect the turrets and hulls of Union monitors. This particular machine was installed at the Continental Ironworks in Greenpoint, New York. Engraving from *Scientific American*, October 25, 1862. (Author's collection)

brought to the Continental Ironworks in Brooklyn, the vessel could be assembled under the supervision of the designer. It was therefore built in a manner which differed from every previous ship construction project. This notion of sub-contracting was repeated in the construction of most subsequent monitors, as foundries specialized in certain aspects, such as engines, turrets or armor plating.

The Continental Ironworks had the ability to forge plate iron into large slabs, but for the construction of most monitors rolled plate was used. It was produced by passing molten iron between two sets of rollers, which formed it into flat sheets. Although the maximum thickness of rolled plate at the time was 2.5 inches, this involved a costly re-configuration of machinery. Consequently, most monitors used a series of 1 inch rolled plates which were laminated together. Flat metal plates could then be shaped by means of a hydraulic ram. Before assembly they were cut and drilled, and each plate was given a reference number, to ensure each piece was fitted exactly where the designer wanted it to go.

Taking the *Monitor* as an example, her keel was laid in a specially constructed assembly shed, and consisted of a series of 7.5 ft long metal plates. The major bottom plates (each 11 ft x 3 ft) were bolted in strakes on each side of the keel, and secured by heated rivets, which tightened the joint as they cooled. The exterior of the lower hull was then surrounded by a 4 ft wide metal plate, secured by angled brackets and set 5 ft below the top of the lower deck structure. In effect it formed an iron shelf, running around the ship. 1 ft square oak beams sat vertically around the shelf, and were bolted to the inner hull. These beams were then covered by horizontally laid pine beams. This wooden backing was finished off by adding five layers of 1 inch thick iron plating, which was bolted in place to complete the lower hull. This ledge of wood and iron formed the side armor of the vessel.

The upper hull was essentially a deck, supported by 10 inch square oak beams and diagonal bracers. This was covered by pine planking, then two layers of $\frac{1}{2}$ inch iron plating, extending over the top of the wood backing until it joined with the layers of hull armor. At the bow and stern, additional "truss frames" supported the deck beams and side armor, as the upper deck extended beyond the lower hull. These also formed protective covers for the propeller assembly and the anchor well.

The turret was constructed by bending a series of 1 inch iron plates, each measuring 9 ft x 3 ft. These were assembled in a workshop around a 20 ft diameter wooden framework, and each layer was drilled to provide holes for rivets. The gunports were also cut out of the appropriate plates. The process was repeated with eight successive layers of plating. The completed structure was then riveted together. The turret construction was then taken to the ship assembly shed and lowered over the hole left in the upper deck. It was secured to a beam that formed the turret base-plate, then reinforced with additional plating. The guns were then lowered into their mountings by crane, and the turret rotation mechanism attached to the baseplate assembly. A ledge around the interior of the turret top was used to support the iron beams that formed the turret roof.

Once the monitor was launched, finishing work took place on interior wooden partitions surrounding the living spaces, and stores, equipment and other small items were added. Once this was finished the vessel was commissioned into service, and a naval crew took over control of the vessel though, in theory, the vessel remained the responsibility of the designer until the captain reported he was happy with the performance of the ship.

Bending 1 in. thick metal plates in a New York foundry, 1862. This particular hydraulic press produced curved plates for gun turrets by applying up to 1,400 tons of pressure to the metal plate. From *Harper's Monthly Magazine*, September 1862. (Author's collection)

BENDING THE PLATES.

MONITORS IN OPERATION

The role of the monitors

The original *Monitor* was designed to fight enemy ironclads but, contrary to his later statements, the designer John Ericsson also claimed the vessel could successfully engage shore batteries. The success of the USS *Monitor* in countering the threat of the CSS *Virginia* led to a gross overestimation of the potential of Ericsson's design. The monitor as a ship type was imbued with qualities that exceeded the limitations of the design. Consequently, when these vessels were sent into action against powerful fortifications such as Fort Sumter and the coastal defenses surrounding Charleston, South Carolina, the result was a near disaster. This debacle led to a re-evaluation of monitor design, but not of the role given to these warships.

As a warship with which to counter the threat of enemy ironclads, the monitor design proved highly successful. The ease with which the Passaic class monitor USS *Weehawken* defeated the casemate ironclad CSS *Atlanta* in June 1863 demonstrated the superiority of these improved versions of the original monitor over Confederate casemate ironclads. This superiority was further demonstrated during the Battle of Mobile Bay in August 1864, when the Milwaukee class monitor USS *Chickasaw* was able to pound the ironclad CSS *Tennessee* into submission. During the Battle of Trent's Reach fought on the James River in January 1865, the twin-turreted monitor USS *Onondaga* clearly outclassed the ironclad CSS *Virginia (II)*.

The weakness of the monitor designs lay in their poor buoyancy and lack of seaworthiness. Given the use of monitors to bolster the blockade of the Confederate coast, it was inevitable that these vessels were placed at risk of loss through rough seas or underwater obstructions. Consequently, of all the operational monitors which were lost during the war, only the USS *Keokuk* sank as a result of enemy fire. The USS *Monitor* and the USS *Weehawken* foundered in rough seas, while the USS *Tecumseh*, the USS *Patapsco* and the USS *Milwaukee* were sunk after hitting enemy torpedoes (mines). No monitor was ever lost or even seriously damaged while in action with an enemy ironclad, while two Confederate ironclads

The USS *Weehawken* depicted in a storm, 1863. The Passaic class monitor played a leading role in the blockade of Charleston but, on the afternoon of December 6, she lay at anchor when a gale sprang up from the north-east. Water flooded in through a forward hatch, and she went down by the bow within five minutes. (Author's collection)

USS Keokuk

USS Weehawken

ft.

m

0   10   20   30   40   50

0   5   10   15

A

B

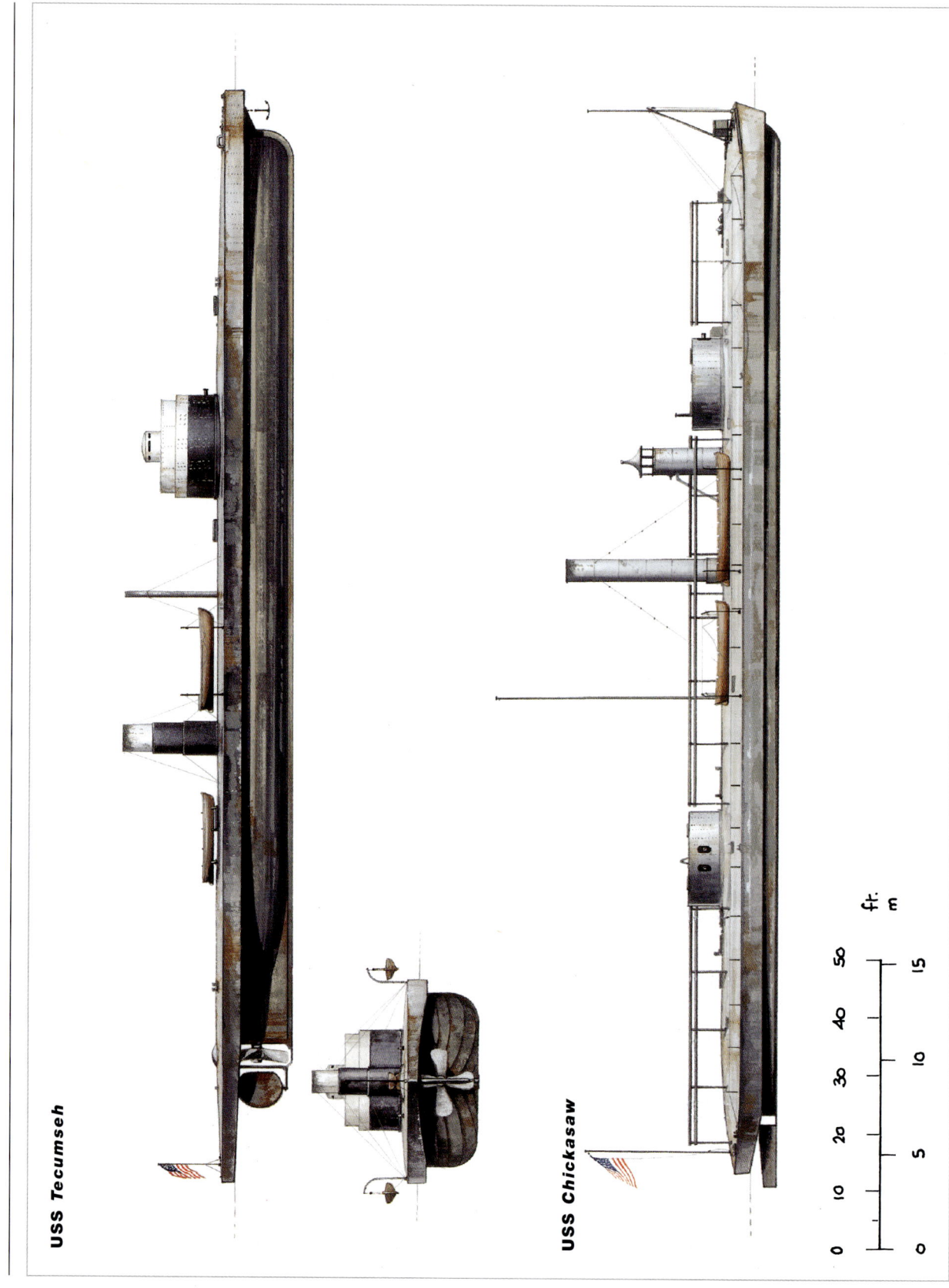

USS Tecumseh

USS Chickasaw

ft.
m

0   10   20   30   40   50

0   5   10   15

The bombardment of Fort Sumter, 1863

C

USS *MONITOR*

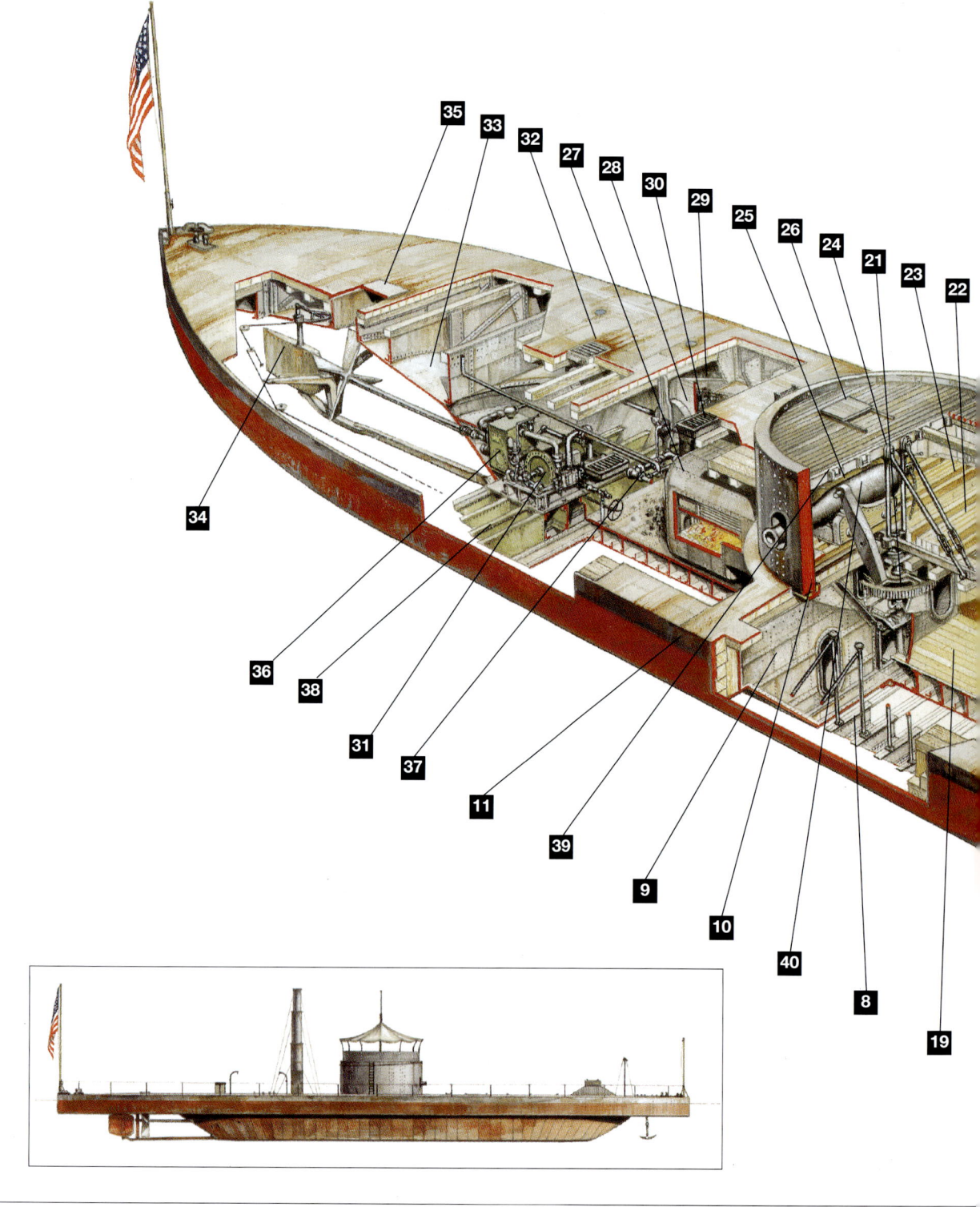

KEY

1. Anchor
2. Anchor Well
3. Boatswain's Locker (both sides)
4. Hand-powered Windlass
5. Chain Locker
6. Tiller Actuating Ropes
7. Timber Deck Beams
8. Deck Beam Supports and Bracings
9. Main Bulkhead
10. Brass Turret Ring
11. Hull Armor
12. Ship's Wheel
13. Observation Slit (0.5 in.)
14. Pilothouse
15. Deck Plating
16. Captain's Cabin (Stateroom on Starboard Side)
17. Officers' State Rooms
18. Store Rooms
19. Crews' Quarters (Berth Deck)
20. Glass Deck Lights (covered in action)
21. Turret Traverse Mechanism
22. Turret Support Beams
23. Gun Carriage Rails
24. Turret Frame Stanchions (2.5 in.)
25. Gunport Stopper (shown open)
26. Turret Hatch (1 of 2)
27. Boiler (1 of 2)
28. Blower Engine (on both sides)
29. Coal Bunker Bulkhead
30. Smokestack (1 of 2)
31. Engine
32. Ventilator
33. Propeller Housing
34. Rudder
35. Propeller Well and Access Hatch
36. Condenser (Starboard side only)
37. Steam Discharge Pipes and Stop Valves
38. Engine Bulkheads
39. Main Turret Beam
40. 11 in. Dahlgren smoothbore

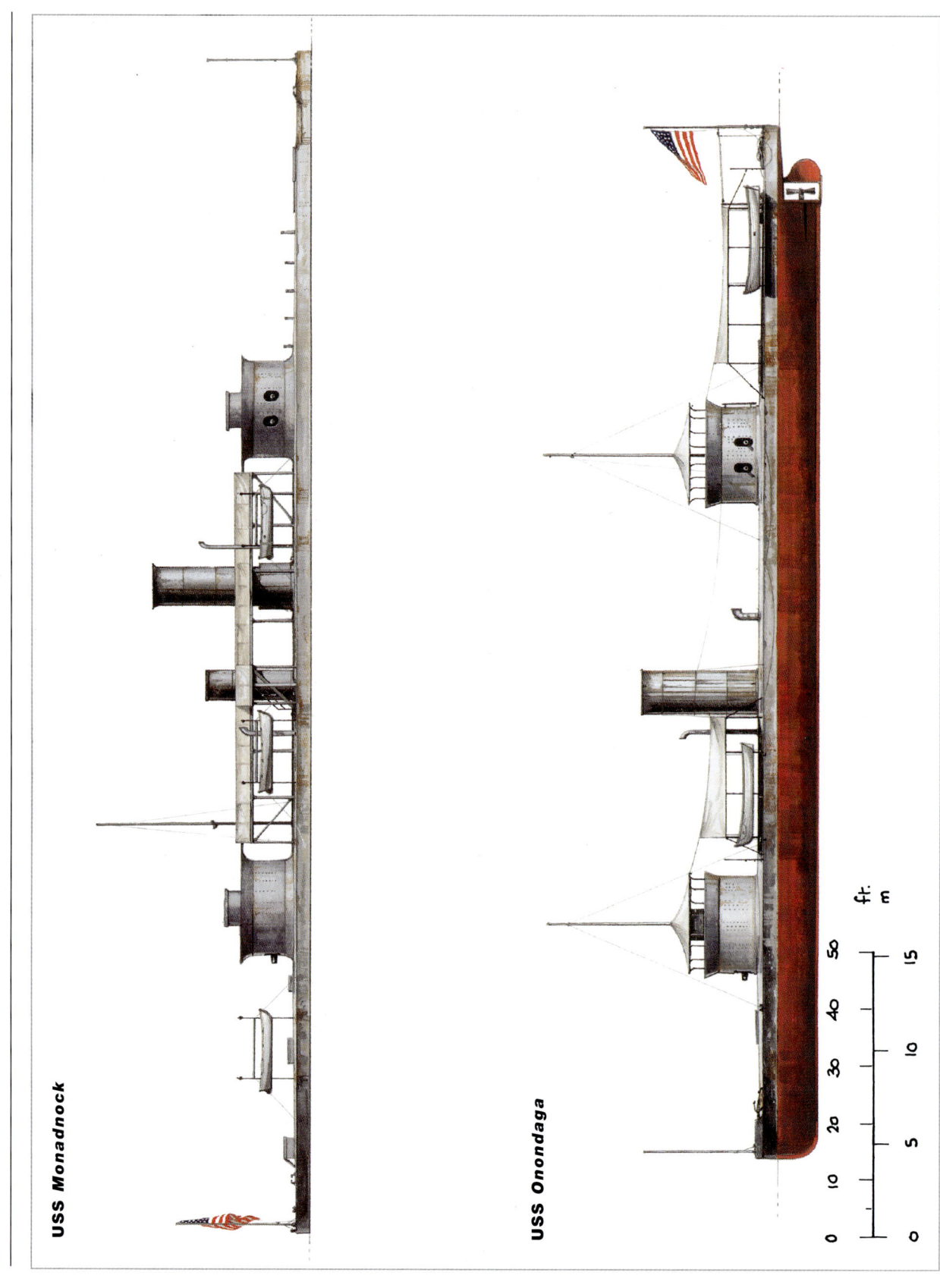

USS *Monadnock*

USS *Onondaga*

ft.
m

0   10   20   30   40   50   ft.
0   5   10   15   m

E

The bombardment of Fort Fisher, 1865

F

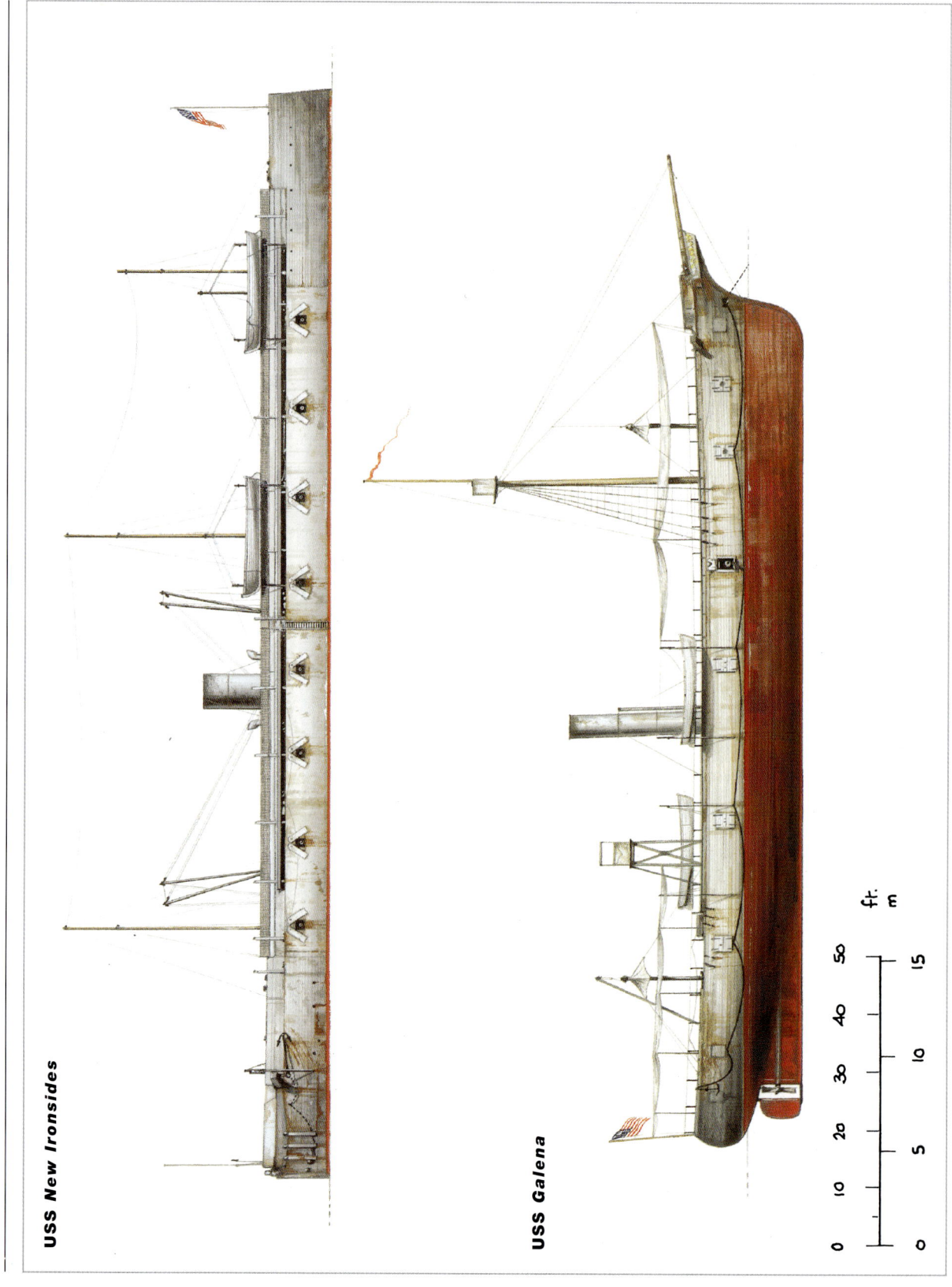

G

USS _New Ironsides_

USS _Galena_

ft.
m

0   10   20   30   40   50
0   5   10   15

were captured following engagements with monitors. This is perhaps the greatest justification for the faith placed by the US Navy in John Ericsson's revolutionary design.

Crewing the monitors

The original *Monitor* had a crew of 58 men. As monitor designs became larger and more complex, the vessels consequently needed increasingly large crews. Passaic and Canonicus class monitors required a crew of 65–88 to operate, while double-turreted monitors such as the USS *Onondaga* required a crew of 130–150, as did the armored gunboat USS *Galena*. The most manpower intensive of the Union ironclads was the USS *New Ironsides*, which had a complement of 460 men. In theory, the USS *Roanoke* had a full complement of 350, but she never received more than a fraction of her full complement because of her limited usefulness.

These crews were divided into two watches in the same manner as the rest of the fleet, and these were further subdivided into divisions, where each was responsible for a particular area of the ship's operation (e.g. turret division or engineering division). Taking the USS *Monitor* as an example, her 58 hands included 13 officers and 45 sailors of various rates. Five of the officers and 17 sailors were engineers, responsible for the operation of the engines and all machinery, including the turret rotation system. A further 5 officers (including the captain) and 21 sailors were "of the line," responsible for gunnery, and all tasks relating to seamanship. The Surgeon and Paymaster were officers without operational duties, while the Ship's Clerk was a petty officer. In addition the crew included seven "waisters," an archaic term applied to the storemen, clerks, cooks and stewards who were not required to keep watches. The quota of officers included 5 ensigns, 3 of whom were engineers. While the crew of the USS *Monitor* were all volunteers, subsequent monitors had their crews drafted to them in the same manner as all other vessels in the fleet.

The crew of the USS *Monitor*, in an engraving based on a photo taken two months after the Battle of Hampton Roads. Although improvements were made to the crew quarters on subsequent monitors, conditions in these ironclads were probably the worst in the entire fleet. (HCA)

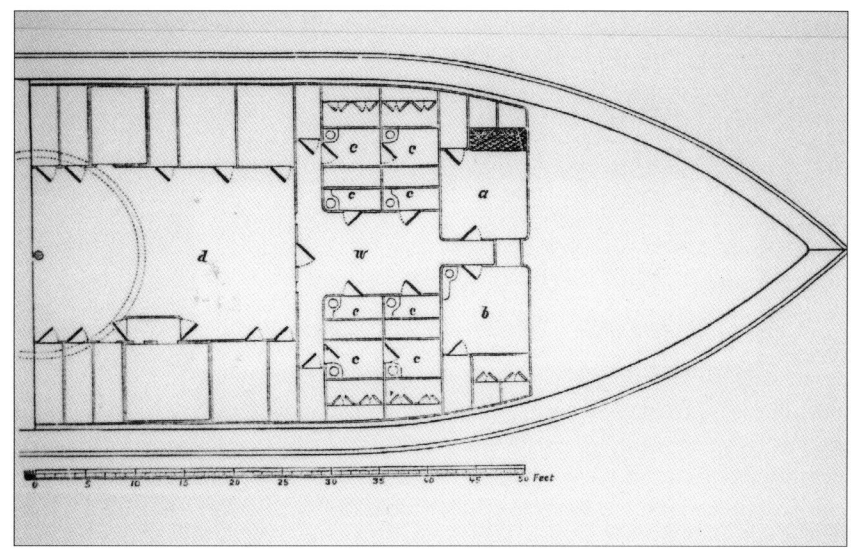

The Line officers were considered superior to the engineers, an elitism which was less pronounced in monitors than in the rest of the fleet because of the inherently technical nature of the vessels themselves. Most officers who served in monitors volunteered to do so, and were therefore more willing to accept the technical aspects of many of their duties which differed from those in conventional warships.

Among the most useful members of the crew were the petty officers, whose ranks included the boatswain, the gunner's mates and the quartermaster, all of whom were set apart in terms of responsibility. In addition these senior rates included skilled machinists and engineers, responsible for the maintenance, operation and repair of the monitor's machinery. For the "black gang" in the engine room, conditions were appalling, with temperatures only partially helped by often inefficient ventilation systems. There was also the near-constant risk of a build-up of poisonous fumes, and during the *Monitor*'s journey to Hampton Roads, fumes forced the abandonment of the engine room for several hours. If conditions were bad for most of the personnel in the engine room, they were worse for the firemen and coal heavers, whose duty was to keep the boiler furnaces trimmed and supplied, two of the dirtiest and most exhausting jobs on board.

When off duty, officers were able to relax in their own private staterooms, while the captain had two such cabins. While the petty officers enjoyed their own communal mess, the rest of the monitor's crew ate, slept and relaxed on the berth deck, which was poorly ventilated and often damp. A common complaint was the heat on board a monitor, particularly during the summer. In winter, the reverse was the case, and only the engine room was comfortably warm. Boredom was also common, particularly when monitors were on blockade. The iron hulls of most monitors "sweated," creating a humid atmosphere below decks. One monitor sailor reported it was like "living in a well." Sailors serving in monitors had to endure these conditions for months on end, but occasionally a monitor would be allowed to put into ports such as New Orleans, Key West or Port Royal for supplies, maintenance, and a "run ashore." For more significant repairs, monitors returned north to

New York, Boston, or some other major port. Although conditions were primitive, service on board a monitor carried with it an element of glamor, as the vessels were almost guaranteed to be in the forefront of any major engagement.

Ordnance and gunnery

By the start of the Civil War, the US Navy was well equipped with ordnance, and throughout the war the service relied exclusively on smoothbore shell guns designed by John Dahlgren and rifled guns designed by Robert Parrott. Apart from a few exceptions, all monitors were fitted with Dahlgren smoothbores.

John A. Dahlgren was a serving naval officer who was assigned to ordnance duty in 1847. He developed a new system of naval ordnance, and produced plans for several new guns. These included his 11 inch and 15 inch smoothbores, but he also developed 12-pounder "boat howitzers" for use against boarders or to arm small launches. In 1861 Commander Dahlgren became commander of the Washington Navy Yard, and in July 1862 he was promoted to captain and named as Chief of the Navy Department's Ordnance Bureau before returning to active service with the fleet in 1863.

Dahlgren's first 9 inch smoothbore shell gun entered service in 1850, and it was easily identifiable through its "soda bottle" shape. The larger guns which Dahlgren installed in Union monitors were simply bigger versions of this weapon. The following year he produced an 11 inch smoothbore, which weighed 15,700 pounds (just over 8 tons) and fired a 135 pound shell. It was also capable of firing a 165 pound solid roundshot. The shot was propelled by a 15 pound charge of powder, but after the guns of the USS *Monitor* failed to penetrate the hull of the CSS *Virginia*, Dahlgren ordered the charge increased to 20–25 pounds, which improved the penetrative power of the shot.

Dahlgren also produced a 10 inch smoothbore for use on a pivot carriage, and the USS *Galena* carried four 9 inch Dahlgrens on similar pivot mounts, designed to fire out of either side of the hull. Conventional warships carried these guns mounted on wooden "Marsilly" carriages, a French design with two front wheels, and these were also used on board the USS *New Ironsides*. Monitors required special treatment, and consequently special sliding carriages were developed by John Ericsson, working in consultation with Dahlgren.

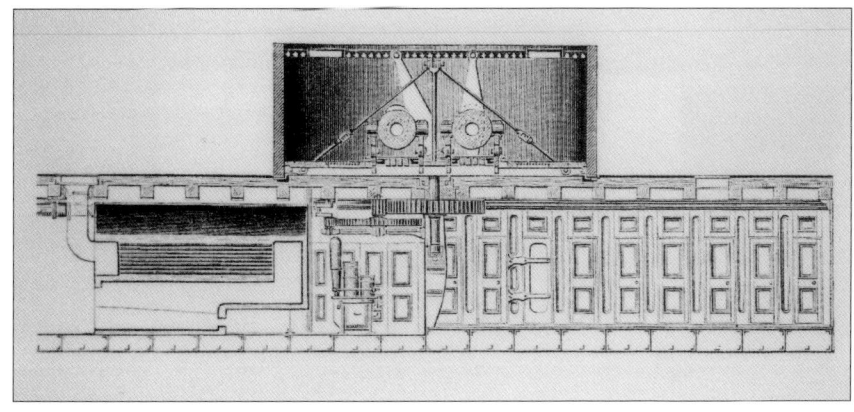

A cross-section of the turret of the USS *Monitor*, showing her 11 in. Dahlgren smoothbore guns run forward into their firing position. Her turret turning mechanism was improved in subsequent monitor designs. (HCA)

Dahlgren was also working on designs for 13 inch, 15 inch and 20 inch smoothbores when the war broke out, and of these, the 15 inch was ready for production, and was rushed into service during 1862. The first became available in September, but technical problems at their foundry prevented them appearing in sufficient quantities until the following year. Consequently, only one of each of these new guns was fitted into the turrets of Passaic class monitors rather than the two which had been planned. These 15 inch guns weighed 42,000 pounds (21 tons), and fired a 330 pound shell or a 440 pound solid shot. The sheer weight of the gun and projectile necessitated the adoption of mechanical loading systems, and again, Ericsson and Dahlgren worked together to produce a viable design, which was introduced into the Passaic class monitors and all subsequent ironclads. While the 11 inch smoothbore could be reloaded in three minutes, the 15 inch piece

Interior view of the turret of a Passaic class monitor, with an 11 in. Dahlgren smoothbore in the foreground, and a 15 in. Dahlgren fitted in the port mounting. Note the method of storing ready-use shot in rings running around the inside of the turret, and the overhead gantry used to load the projectiles into the guns. (HCA)

required 5–6 minutes. Also, the 11 inch was designed to be fired by a crew of 16 men, although it could be operated by a crew of eight. The 15 inch smoothbore normally needed a crew of 14 men, which would have led to overcrowding within the turret. By relying on mechanical aids, the gun could be operated by a crew of eight men. The largest Dahlgren to enter production was the 20 inch smoothbore, which weighed 100,000 pounds, and these were available to the navy by late 1864. Although Ericsson planned to fit two of these guns into his ocean-going monitor *Puritan*, the vessel never entered service.

In 1861, Robert P. Parrott had designed a series of small rifled guns for naval use, including a 100 pounder (6.4 inch) rifle. By the end of the year his 150 pounder (8 inch) Parrott rifle entered service. The US Army classified the same weapon as a 200 pounder Parrott rifle. It fired a 152 pound shell over five miles, which was approximately four times the range of an 11 inch Dahlgren. Despite these figures the principle of rifling a gun had never been fully accepted in the pre-war US Navy, as naval tacticians emphasized weight of firepower over range and accuracy. While the Confederate Navy relied on rifled guns to provide the principal armament in their ironclads, the Union Navy tended to avoid these weapons, and instead relied on the immense battering power of Dahlgren's smoothbores.

The only coastal monitor to carry rifled guns was the USS *Roanoke*, and she never saw active service. The USS *Galena* carried two 100 pounder Parrott rifled guns, while the USS *New Ironsides* was armed with two 150 pounder rifles and two 50 pounders in addition to her main battery of 11 inch Dahlgren smoothbores. Unlike Dahlgren's guns which were completely reliable, Parrott rifles were occasionally prone to bursting, and following an incident on the *New Ironsides* during the bombardment of Fort Fisher, the 150 pounder guns were withdrawn from service. Dahlgren also designed 50 pounder rifled guns.

Due to the restricted space inside a gun turret, mechanical aids were used to perform many gunnery functions. Pulleys were used to raise port stoppers, and hand-cranks were used to run the guns out and in. Guns were trained by rotating the turret, and at action stations an engineer was detailed to operate the crank inside the turret which engaged the turret rotation system. It was found it was often difficult to stop the turret turning when the enemy was on target, so the gun was sometimes fired while the turret was still in motion. After firing the turret was normally trained fore and aft to allow powder and shot to be passed up from the magazine, although a small ready-use supply was stored inside the turret itself. An overhead gantry

The interior plan of the turret of a Canonicus class monitor. The turret interior of a Passaic class monitor was similar, except the right-hand gun was an 11 in. piece. The two 15 in. Dahlgren smoothbores are shown run back for reloading. An overhead gantry was used to load the projectiles. Engraving from "US Navy Ordnance Instructions, 1866." (Author's collection)

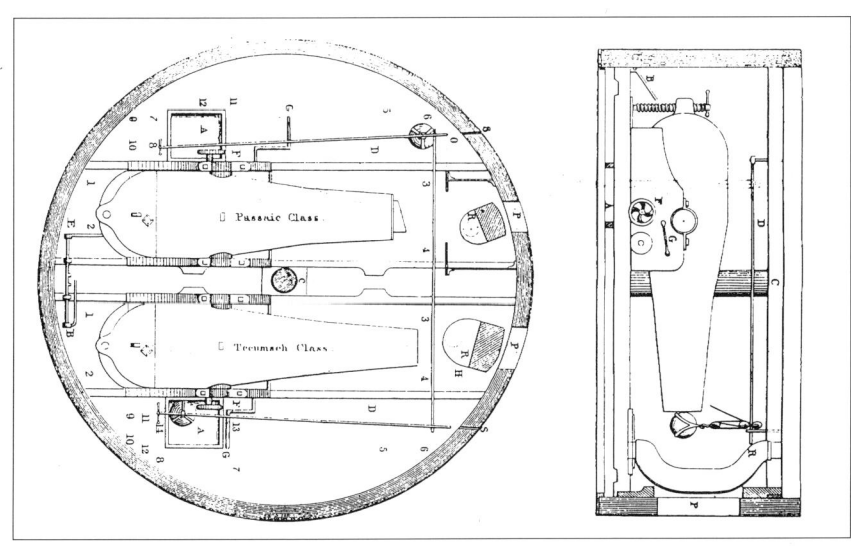

was used to transport the shot of a 15 inch gun across the turret to the muzzle, but 11 inch shot was loaded by hand, using a shot holder, which resembled a small stretcher, carried by two men. In action the smoke, noise and confusion must have been indescribable, and it was easy for the gunnery officer in charge of the turret to become disorientated. On monitors where the pilothouse was fitted over the turret (it remained stationary through its attachment to a central spindle), the control of the gun was far easier, as the helmsman was able to confirm when the guns were facing the target.

Monitors in action

Naval officers were unable to draw on any body of tactical experience when the war began. The only naval tactical manuals available which were relevant in an age of rapid technological change were of little use to the commanders of the Union monitors. All that commanders like Lieutenant John Worden of the USS *Monitor* had to base their tactics on were the claims of designers such as Ericsson and their own common sense.

During the Battle of Hampton Roads, Worden decided to take advantage of his warship's maneuverability, and the ability of his guns to fire regardless of the direction his ship was heading. The only blocked field of fire was directly forward to prevent damage to the pilothouse. Worden chose to circle his opponent, firing his guns at as close a range as possible. In action he found his guns could fire every eight minutes, a significantly slower rate of fire than expected. After the first few shots the gun crew discovered the stratagem of leaving the cumbersome port stoppers open, and turning the turret away from the enemy to reload. As bearing marks inside the turret were quickly obliterated, it became almost impossible to aim the turret with any degree of accuracy. Lieutenant Dana Greene elected to fire "on the fly," rotating the turret until the *Virginia* became visible through an open gunport, then firing one of the guns. This meant that Greene was able to hit the target with almost every shot, but it also made it virtually impossible to concentrate fire on one particular spot on the *Virginia*'s casemate. Although fire from the *Virginia* struck the turret, the shots were unable to penetrate the armor. To ensure communications between the turret and the pilothouse, Lieutenant Keeler and a clerk ran back and forth between the two locations with messages. After almost four hours of fighting, a rifled shell from the *Virginia* struck the *Monitor*'s pilothouse and exploded, wounding Worden and tearing away part of the protective armor. Greene soon took over command of the ship, but by that time the *Virginia* had withdrawn back to Norfolk.

The action was studied by other future monitor commanders, and when the Passaic class vessels entered service, their officers knew what they might expect. The engagement between the USS *Weehawken* (supported by the USS *Nahant*) and the casemate ironclad CSS *Atlanta* was a brief, one-sided battle. The *Atlanta* ran aground while

John L. Worden, the captain of the USS *Monitor*, was the first man to command such a vessel in action, and was wounded during the engagement with the CSS *Virginia*. His after-action report was crucial to the modification of subsequent monitor designs. He went on to command the USS *Montauk* off Charleston, and eventually became an admiral. (HCA)

During the attack on Fort Sumter launched by Admiral Du Pont on April 7, 1863, eight Passaic class monitors accompanied by USS *Keokuk* and USS *New Ironsides* bombarded the fort, but were forced to withdraw due to Confederate fire. Until the attack on Fort Fisher two years later the engagement saw the largest deployment of monitors in action. (HCA)

maneuvering for position, and the *Weehawken* captained by Commander Rodgers closed to within 300 yards, taking up a raking position which prevented the Confederates from returning fire with more than one rifled gun. The seven hits scored by the rifle failed to penetrate the monitor, but the *Weehawken*'s 11 inch and 15 inch guns hit the enemy ironclad four times, twice with each gun. Both of the 15 inch shots caused penetrating damage to the *Atlanta*, and she surrendered within 15 minutes. The effectiveness of Dahlgren's smoothbore guns firing heavy solid shot was clearly demonstrated in the engagement, and consequently roundshot was considered the projectile of choice against enemy ironclads.

During the Battle of Mobile Bay in August 1864, the ironclad CSS *Tennessee* was effectively pinned by wooden warships, allowing the USS *Chickasaw* to take up a raking position 50 yards from the enemy's stern. Fire from her 11 inch guns tore away parts of the *Tennessee*'s armor plating, and sent chunks of backing timber scything through the casemate. The *Tennessee* duly surrendered. During the Battle of Trent's Reach on the James River, the USS *Onondaga* fired solid shot from her 15 inch guns at the CSS *Virginia (II)*, scoring two hits which penetrated the ironclad's armor. The engagement proved without doubt that, ship for ship, the monitor design was superior to the casemate ironclad, especially if the Union vessel carried 15 inch guns.

The performance of monitors against static fortifications was less impressive. During Admiral Du Pont's attack on Fort Sumter in April 1863, only the USS *New Ironsides* proved herself to be virtually invulnerable to enemy fire. The Confederates poured shot into the fleet, and an officer on the USS *Passaic* reported that 15 shots passed his ship in the opening seconds of the battle. She was struck 36 times during the engagement, while the USS *Weehawken* suffered 53 hits, two more than the USS *Nantucket*. All these shots dented the armor of the various turrets, but none of them penetrated, although several injuries were caused by concussion. If a crewman happened to be leaning against the turret side when it was hit, he could be seriously injured or even killed by the concussion. Despite this, Ericsson's armored plate functioned well under what was probably its most severe test of the war. Two turrets were jammed by enemy shot striking the join between the turret and the deck, effectively putting the ships out of action. Two other monitors suffered hits to their guns, which damaged them and put them out of action.

The USS *Monitor* sank in a gale off Cape Hatteras in late December 1862. In this engraving the USS *Rhode Island* is shown coming to the aid of the sinking vessel. All but 16 of her crew were rescued before the *Monitor* foundered. (HCA)

The lessons learned that day bore fruit when the monitor fleet was given the task of bombarding Fort Fisher. This time each vessel was assigned specific targets, such as individual embrasures. Although on the first day the USS *Canonicus* was hit 36 times, no serious damage was inflicted, largely due to the protective glacis that had been fitted around the turret. By contrast, almost every gun in the fort was dismounted and damaged during the bombardment. To cause maximum damage, monitors first fired one of their guns at a target, which inevitably drove the defenders behind cover. The gunners would then wait until the Confederates re-emerged before firing again. Although monitors were ill-designed for fighting powerful shore fortifications, and fire from Confederate positions regularly struck the ships, no monitor was ever seriously damaged in a bombardment, although the casemate ironclad *Keokuk* sank as a result of enemy fire. After modifications to the turret protection of the Passaic class, monitors were virtually invulnerable to enemy fire, and could inflict far more damage to enemy fortifications than they received.

CATALOG OF OCEAN-GOING UNION MONITORS

Although the Milwaukee class ships were not designed as ocean-going monitors, they have been included in this list because two of the class joined the ocean-going Gulf Blockading Squadron, and participated in the Battle of Mobile Bay in 1864. Also, although the USS *New Ironsides* and USS *Galena* were not monitors, they have been included as they were ocean-going ironclads, and fought alongside monitors in action. Similarly the spar torpedo boat USS *Spuyten Duyvil* has been included as it was of ironclad construction, and supported the monitor USS *Onondaga* during the Battle of Trent's Reach in 1865.

All other Union monitors and casemate ironclads were not ocean-going vessels, and will form part of a later Osprey study.

MONITOR

Built:	New York, NY
Displacement:	987 tons
Dimensions:	179 ft × 41 ft 6 in. × 10 ft 6 in.
Speed:	9 knots
Armament:	2 × 11 in. smoothbores in a single turret
Armor:	9 in. pilothouse, 8 in. turret, 4.5 in. hull, 2 in. deck
Crew:	49
Service:	Commissioned February 1862; foundered December 31, 1862

GALENA

Built:	Mystic, CT
Displacement:	950 tons
Dimensions:	210 ft × 36 ft × 12 ft 8 in.
Speed:	8 knots
Armament:	2 × 100 pdr rifles + 4 × 9 in. smoothbores, broadside mounted, capable of firing to either side
Armor:	3.5 in. hull, unarmored deck
Crew:	150
Service:	Commissioned April 1862

NEW IRONSIDES

Built:	Philadelphia, PA
Displacement:	4,120 tons
Dimensions:	232 ft × 57 ft 6 in. × 15 ft 8 in.
Speed:	6 knots
Armament:	2 × 150 pdr rifles + 14 × 11 in. smoothbores, broadside mounted, capable of firing to one side only
Armor:	10 in. pilothouse, 3–4.5 in. hull, 1 in. deck
Crew:	460
Service:	Commissioned August 1862

ROANOKE

Built:	New York, NY (Converted from steam frigate)
Displacement:	6,300 tons
Dimensions:	278 ft × 52 ft 6 in × 24 ft 3 in.
Speed:	6 knots
Armament:	1 × 15 in. smoothbore + 1 × 150 pdr rifle (forward turret) 1 × 15 in. smoothbore + 1 × 11 in. smoothbore (middle turret) 1 × 11 in. smoothbore + 1 × 150 pdr rifle (after turret)
Armor:	9 in. pilothouse, 11 in. turrets, 4.5 in. casemate, 3 in. hull, 2.5 in. deck
Crew:	350
Service:	Commissioned June 1863; re-designated a harbor-defense vessel Hampton Roads July 1863

KEOKUK

Built:	New York, NY
Displacement:	677 tons
Dimensions:	159 ft 6 in. × 36 ft × 8 ft 6 in.
Speed:	9 knots
Armament:	2 × 11 in. smoothbores on pivot mounts in two casemates
Armor:	4 in. hull and deck, 4.5 in. turrets and pilothouse
Crew:	92
Service:	Commissioned March 1863; foundered April 8, 1863

PASSAIC CLASS

10 in class

Built:	Jersey City, NJ (2), New York, NY (3), Philadelphia, PA (2), Boston, MA (2), Wilmington, DE (1)
Displacement:	1,335 tons
Dimensions:	200 ft × 46 ft × 11 ft 6 in.
Speed:	7 knots
Armament:	1 × 15 in. smoothbore + 1 × 11 in. smoothbore in a single turret (except Camanche 2 × 15 in. smoothbores)
Armor:	8 in. pilothouse, 11 in. turret, 5 in. hull, 1 in. deck
Crew:	67–88
Service	
Passaic:	Commissioned November 1862
Montauk:	Commissioned December 1862
Nahant:	Commissioned December 1862
Patapsco:	Commissioned January 1863; sunk by torpedo January 16, 1865
Weehawken:	Commissioned January 1863; foundered December 6, 1863
Sangamon:	Commissioned February 1863
Catskill:	Commissioned February 1863
Nantucket:	Commissioned February 1863
Lehigh:	Commissioned April 1863
Camanche:	Commissioned May 1865

CANONICUS CLASS

5 in class during war, plus 4 built after war ended

Built:	Jersey City, NJ (3), Boston, MA (1), Wilmington, DE (1)
Displacement:	2,100 tons
Dimensions:	223 ft × 43 ft 4 in. × 13 ft 6 in. (Saugus and Canonicus were 235 ft × 43 ft 8 in. × 13 ft 6in)
Speed:	8 knots
Armament:	2 × 15 in. smoothbores in a single turret
Armor:	11 in. turret and pilothouse, 5 in. hull, 1.5 in. deck
Crew:	85
Service	
Canonicus:	Commissioned April 1864
Saugus:	Commissioned April 1864
Tecumseh:	Commissioned April 1864; sunk by torpedo August 5, 1864
Manhattan:	Commissioned June 1864
Mahopac:	Commissioned September 1864

Catawba, Manaynuck, Oneota, and Tippecanoe were completed after the war ended

DICTATOR

Built:	New York, NY
Displacement:	4,438 tons
Dimensions:	312 ft × 50 ft × 20 ft 6 in.
Speed:	9 knots
Armament:	2 × 15 in. smoothbores in a single turret
Armor:	15 in. turret, 12 in. pilothouse, 6 in. hull, 1.5 in. deck
Crew:	174
Service:	Commissioned November 1864

ONONDAGA

Built:	New York, NY
Displacement:	2,592 tons
Dimensions:	226 ft × 49 ft 3 in. × 12 ft 10 in.
Speed:	7 knots
Armament:	2 × 8 in. rifles in forward turret + 2 × 15 in. smoothbores in after turret
Armor:	11.75 in. turrets and pilothouse, 5.5 in. hull, 1 in. deck
Crew:	130
Service:	Commissioned March 1864

MONADNOCK CLASS

2 in class

Built:	*Monadnock* Boston, MA; *Agamenticus* Portsmouth, ME
Displacement:	3,295 tons
Dimensions:	250 ft × 53 ft 8 in. × 12 ft 3 in.
Speed:	9 knots
Armament:	4 × 15 in. smoothbores in two turrets (two guns per turret)
Armor:	11 in. turrets, 8 in. pilothouse, 4.5 in. hull, 1.5 in. deck
Crew:	130
Service	
Monadnock:	Commissioned October 1864
Agamenticus:	Commissioned May 1865

SPUYTEN DUYVIL

Built:	Mystic, CT
Displacement:	207 tons
Dimensions:	84 ft 2 in. × 20 ft 8 in. × 7 ft 6 in.
Speed:	5 knots
Armament:	One spar torpedo
Armor:	5 in. pilothouse, 5 in. hull, 3 in. deck
Crew:	23
Service:	Commissioned October 1864

MILWAUKEE CLASS

4 built during war

Built:	Carondelet, MO
Displacement:	1,300 tons
Dimensions:	229 ft × 56 ft 8 in. × 6 ft
Speed:	9 knots
Armament:	4 × 11 in. smoothbores in two turrets (two guns per turret)
Armor:	8 in. turrets and pilothouse, 4 in. hull, 1.5 in. deck
Crew:	138
Service	
Winnebago:	Commissioned April 1864
Chickasaw:	Commissioned May 1864
Kickapoo:	Commissioned July 1864
Milwaukee:	Commissioned August 1864; sunk by torpedo March 18, 1865

CASCO CLASS

4 in class during war, 16 built after war ended

Built:	*Casco, Chimo* Boston, MA; *Tunxis* Chester, PA; *Naubuc* Williamsburg, NY
Displacement:	1,175 tons
Dimensions:	225 ft × 45 ft × 9 ft
Speed:	9 knots
Armament:	*Casco, Naubuc* 1 × 11 in. smoothbore on an open pivot mount, spar torpedo; *Tunxis* 1 × 11 in. smoothbore and one 150 pdr rifle in a single turret; *Chimo* 1 × 150 pdr rifle
Armor:	10 in. pilothouse, 3 in. hull and deck; *Tunxis* 8 in. turret
Crew:	69
Service	
Casco:	Commissioned April 1864
Tunxis:	Commissioned July 1864
Chimo:	Commissioned January 1865
Naubuc:	Commissioned March 1865

Cohoes, Etlah, Klamath, Koka, Modoc, Napa, Nausett, Shawnee, Shiloh, Squando, Suncook, Umpqua, Wassuc, Waxhaw, Yazoo, and *Yuma* were completed after the war ended, and most were never commissioned.

Ships not commissioned
The following ships were ordered during the war, but were never commissioned before the war ended.

Puritan
Monitor type; 2 x 20 in. smoothbores in a single turret. Built in Greenpoint, NY, she was launched in July 1864, but construction was suspended following the end of the war.

Dundenberg
Casemate ironclad; 4 x 15 in. smoothbores, 8 x 11 in. smoothbores, broadside mounted. Built in Greenpoint, NY, she was laid down in October 1862, but was not launched until after the end of the war. She was never completed or commissioned, but was sold to the French Navy in 1867.

Miantonomoh
Monitor type; 4 x 15 in. smoothbores in two turrets (two guns per turret). Built in Brooklyn, NY, she was launched in August 1863, but commissioned after the end of the war.

Tonawanda
Monitor type; 4 x 15 in. smoothbores in two turrets (two guns per turret). Built in Philadelphia, PA, she was launched in May 1864, but commissioned after the end of the war. She was renamed *Amphrite* in 1869.

Kalamazoo class
4 in class (*Kalamazoo, Passaconaway, Quinsigamond* and *Shakamaxon*); monitor type; 4 x 15 in. smoothbores in two turrets (two guns per turret). Built in various ports from Portsmouth to Philadelphia, they were laid down but never launched and scrapped while still on the stocks.

BIBLIOGRAPHY

The following readily available books are recommended for those interested in further reading on the subject. Canney's *Lincoln's Navy* contains a more extensive listing of relevant publications.

Canney, Donald L., *Lincoln's Navy: The Ships, Men and Organisation, 1861–65*, Conway Maritime Press, 1998

Canney, Donald L., *The Old Steam Navy* [2 volumes], Naval Institute Press, 1990 & 1993

Rush, Richard (ed.), *Official Records of the Union and Confederate Navies in the War of the Rebellion* [30 volumes], Government Printing Office, 1895–1921

Silverstone, Paul H., *Warships of the Civil War Navies*, Naval Institute Press, 1989

COLOR PLATE COMMENTARY

PLATE A
USS *Keokuk*

C. W. Whitney of New York designed this unusual ironclad, which proved to be one of the least successful vessels commissioned into the Union fleet. Whitney was a former partner of John Ericsson, the designer of the *Monitor*, but he lacked the Swedish engineer's flair for invention. *Keokuk* used an experimental armor scheme with a "sandwich" of 1 in. iron plates enclosing a 2 in. inner layer of wood, secured in vertical strips onto a thin wooden framework. These were then covered with a skin of boiler plate which was less than 0.5 in. thick. Her ordnance was carried in two casemates which resembled turrets, but were in fact immobile. Each carried an 11 in. Dahlgren smoothbore, capable of firing out of three fixed gunports (two broadside ports and one facing the bow or stern). She soon proved to be hopelessly under-protected.

The Passaic class monitor USS *Montauk* beached for repairs in March 1863, after she was damaged by a mine during the expedition up Georgia's Ogeechee River in late February. The damage was repaired in time for the *Montauk* to participate in the attack on Fort Sumter a month later. (HCA)

In February 1863 she joined the Union squadron off Charleston and under the command of Commander A. D. Rhind she participated in the attack on Fort Sumter in April. She was hit 90 times and, riddled with shot, she limped away from the action. She continued to take on water and sank the following day.

USS *Weehawken*

Following the success of the original *Monitor*, ten similar vessels were ordered, although the design would incorporate several improvements on the original vessel. In effect, the *Monitor* was a prototype for these vessels, which became known as the Passaic class. The greatest improvement was the mounting of the pilothouse over the turret, ensuring constant communication between the captain, the helmsman and the gun crews. The vessels were designed to carry two 15 in. Dahlgren

smoothbores, but a shortage of ordnance forced the fitting of one 11 in. gun in place of a larger piece. USS *Camanche* was armed with two 15 in. guns, but the remainder retained their original armament throughout the war. Under the command of Commander John Rodgers the USS *Weehawken* participated in the attack on Fort Sumter in April 1863 when she was hit 53 times without suffering serious damage. Together with the USS Nahant she captured the ironclad CSS *Atlanta* in June 1863, and bombarded Fort Sumter and Fort Fisher in late 1863. She foundered during a storm off Morris Island, near Charleston, on December 6, 1863.

PLATE B
USS *Tecumseh*

The USS *Tecumseh* was one of the nine vessels of the Canonicus class, five of which were commissioned before the war ended. The class was effectively an enlarged version of the Passaic class. Designed by John Ericsson, these vessels incorporated improvements over their predecessors, including the introduction of finer lines (giving an improved performance), thicker armor, a more efficient turret traversing mechanism and a low glacis protecting the vulnerable junction between the turret and the deck. Like the Passaic

The exterior of the turret of the USS *Monitor* photographed two months after the Battle of Hampton Roads. The improved sloping armor around the pilothouse can be seen behind the turret. (Naval Institute)

class monitors, vessels of the Canonicus class had the pilothouse mounted on top of the turret. The smokestack was retractable, which reduced the risk of damage. In addition, these monitors were fitted with a ventilation system, making living conditions relatively bearable compared to other ironclads of the period. The *Tecumseh* was commissioned in April, 1864, and first saw service on the James River near Richmond before being sent south to join the Gulf Blockading Squadron gathered off Mobile Bay. On August 5, 1864, she led the vanguard of Admiral Farragut's fleet as it forced its way into the bay, but the monitor struck a torpedo (mine), and sank within minutes. Most of her crew were lost, including her commander, Captain Craven.

USS *Chickasaw*

The USS *Chickasaw* was a shallow-drafted river monitor of the Milwaukee class, a double turret design developed by James Eads for use on the Mississippi River. Built in Cincinnatti, the monitor carried four 11 inch Dahlgren smoothbores, mounted two to each turret. The after turret was a standard Ericsson model, but the forward turret was designed by Eads, and was completely steam-operated, a novel design which proved highly effective. Both the USS *Chickasaw* and her sister the USS *Winnebago* saw service during the Battle of Mobile Bay (1864), and served in the Western Gulf Blockading Squadron. Thus, although designed for use on inland rivers, they proved seaworthy enough for use in coastal waters.

PLATE C
The bombardment of Fort Sumter, 1863

On April 7, 1863, Admiral Du Pont launched the Union ironclad fleet against the defenses of Charleston Harbor. The key to the Confederate defense was Fort Sumter, blocking the central channel into the harbor. Du Pont had nine ironclads at his disposal; his flagship the USS *New Ironsides*, seven monitors of the Passaic class (*Weehawken*, *Passaic*, *Montauk*, *Patapsco*, *Catskill*, *Nantucket*, and *Nahant*), and the unique USS *Keokuk*. The admiral formed his fleet into a single line, placing his flagship in its center. The lead ship was the USS *Weehawken*, commanded by Captain John Rodgers. Rodgers advanced north up the main ship channel,

approaching within 500 yards of Fort Sumter around 2.30 pm before the garrison opened fire. As he drew abreast of the fort he spotted a line of barrels ahead of him, which he surmised were torpedoes (mines). He stopped his ship, which plunged the line behind him into disarray. Communications had almost completely broken down, and after three hours, as the monitors began suffering heavy damage, Du Pont was forced to steam to the head of the line so he could order a withdrawal. The order was given at 5.30 pm, and the Union ironclads limped out of range. Some 439 shots from Fort Sumter and nearby Fort Moultrie had struck the fleet, and the USS Keokuk was almost sinking. The flagship alone was hit 93 times, but the total casualties belied the ferocity of the fighting. Only one Union sailor was killed and 22 injured, but there was no doubt that the action was an unmitigated disaster for the Union monitors.

The plate depicts the scene shortly after the Weehawken halted, then backed away from the line of suspected torpedoes. Rodgers' monitor is shown in the foreground, while the damaged *Keokuk* lies between her and the fort. The remainder of the Union fleet is shown in line astern, exchanging shots with the garrison.

PLATE D
USS *Monitor*

The USS *Monitor* was the forerunner of the US Navy's seagoing ironclad fleet. Designed by Swedish-born engineer John Ericsson, she was unlike any other warship that came before, and to many she was more a floating gun turret than a real combatant. She proved her worth during her one-day engagement with the CSS *Virginia*. Although later monitors were larger, better protected and carried a heavier armament, the USS *Monitor* was assured of her place in history as the most celebrated participant in the first battle between two ironclad warships. She was built specifically to counter the development of Confederate ironclads, and when she engaged Confederate batteries at Drewry's Bluff (May 15, 1862) her lack of deck protection left her vulnerable to enemy fire. During the summer of 1862 the *Monitor* was modified to incorporate improvements suggested by her officers. These included the addition of a sloped glacis to protect the pilothouse and a raised and linked smokestack. She foundered in a storm off Cape Hatteras on December 31, 1862, while she was being towed south to join the Union squadron off Charleston. The wreck now forms a protected Federal Marine Sanctuary.

PLATE E
USS *Monadnock*
The creation of a twin-turreted ironclad was the next logical step in the development of the monitor. USS *Monadnock* and her sister-ship *Agamenticus* were laid down in 1862, based on a design by John Lenthall, the Chief of the Bureau of Construction and Repair. Only the *Monadnock* saw service in the war, as her sister was only commissioned in May 1865.

The *Monadnock* was wooden hulled, which meant she could be built at the navy's Portsmouth Navy Yard in New Hampshire rather than in a specialist private yard. She was commissioned in October 1864, allowing her to participate in the bombardment of Fort Fisher in December 1864 and

The USS *New Ironsides* shown after her masts and rigging were removed, and her smokestack was cut down. Although she was sluggish, under-powered and difficult to handle by engines alone, her commander viewed the masts as an encumbrance in battle. (Private collection)

January 1865. Although criticized because her wooden hull was rotten, she confounded her critics after the war by sailing to San Francisco around Cape Horn in 1865. She remained in service for another two decades.

USS *Onondaga*
The USS *Onondaga* was ordered in 1862 and built by her designer, George W. Quintard, at the Continental Ironworks at Greenpoint, New York. The engine was produced under a separate contract in another New York foundry. She was designed to carry one 15 in. Dahlgren smoothbore in each of her Ericsson-designed turrets, alongside an 8 in. rifle, making her unique in the fleet for having mixed rifled and smoothbore guns in her turrets, an attempt to counter the Confederate reliance on rifled guns in their ironclads. Just before she entered service her 8 in. guns were replaced by more powerful 150 pdr rifles. Commissioned in the spring of 1864, she served on the James River, and participated in the Battle of Trent's Reach (January 24, 1865), although she also fought in several less spectacular engagements against Confederate batteries. Following the end of the war she was decommissioned and was subsequently sold to France. Her successful transatlantic passage proved her basic seaworthiness, despite her low freeboard.

PLATE F
The bombardment of Fort Fisher, 1865
By the end of 1864, Wilmington remained the only significant port on the Atlantic seaboard which remained in Confederate hands. The port lay on the Cape Fear River, whose mouth was protected by Fort Fisher. Built on a sand spit, the

A contemporary watercolor sketch by R. G. Skeret of the ironclad gunboat USS *Galena*. The sketch was made shortly after her abortive attack on the Confederate batteries on Drewry's Bluff on the James River, and the damage inflicted to her has not been fully repaired. (USN)

imposing fortification used sand earthworks to form the strongest defensive position in the Confederacy, with 44 heavy guns, guarded by minefields and trenches. It was garrisoned by 1,500 men, commanded by Colonel William Lamb. A Union fleet of 60 vessels was assembled to attack the fortress in late 1864, the largest naval concentration undertaken during the war. An initial assault was made on Christmas Day 1864, the land attack supported by a devastating naval bombardment. The attack was repulsed, giving the garrison a brief respite, but two weeks later the fleet returned. On January 13, 1865, the Union warships began a non-stop bombardment of Fort Fisher which lasted for 60 hours. The 40,000 shells and mortar bombs fired into the position destroyed many of the gun positions and caused over 300 casualties. The non-stop bombardment also demoralized the garrison, and prevented any return fire, as the defenders were forced to take shelter in their earthworks. On the afternoon of January 15 a force of 8,000 Union troops assaulted the fort, coming under heavy canister and rifle fire during their advance across the open neck of the sand spit. Despite heavy casualties the attackers entered the fort, and after a bitter hand-to-hand struggle lasting into the night the defenders were forced to surrender. A week later Wilmington fell to the Union, and the Confederacy was finally cut off from the sea.

The plate depicts the situation on January 14, when the fort had been subjected to constant bombardment for over a day. While the more vulnerable wooden warships remained at extreme range, the division of a dozen ironclads maintained a position 500–600 yards from the earthworks, while a squadron of four monitors positioned themselves between the line of ironclads and the shore. The USS *New Ironsides* is shown in the foreground, with the USS *Canonicus* astern of her. Between these ironclads and the shore the USS *Mahopac* is shown leading the inshore squadron.

PLATE G
USS *New Ironsides*
The USS *New Ironsides* was commissioned as a prototype, and her armored casemate design was effectively a copy of that of the French ocean-going ironclad, the *Gloire*. Ordered at the same time as Ericsson's *Monitor*, the vessel presented a viable alternative to the monitor concept. She may have become the pattern for further Union ironclads, but after the Battle of Hampton Roads (1862) when "monitor fever" swept the North, only improved versions of the monitor design were ordered. The vessel had a protected casemate (or battery box) of 4.5 in. of forged metal plating backed by 15 in. of wood, making her one of the best protected warships in the fleet. She was also one of the best armed, carrying 16 heavy guns, including two rifles. Although her engines were under-powered, her sailing rig was removed soon after she was commissioned, as her commanders recognized that the masts were little more than a liability in action. This awkward vessel served as a flagship for the Atlantic Blockading Squadron, and spent most of her wartime career off Charleston, then participated in the bombardment of Fort Fisher.

USS *Galena*
A second alternative to the monitor design was the gunboat USS *Galena*, which carried a 3 in. protective layer of steel planking secured to her hull, with a pronounced tumblehome to encourage the deflection of enemy shot. Built at the Maxson Fish Yard in Mystic, Connecticut, according to a design devised by S. H. Pook, she was commissioned in April 1862, and saw action less than a month later at Drewry's Bluff, below Richmond, Virginia. Her armor proved woefully inadequate against plunging fire from the bluff, and she was withdrawn from active service. Her armor was removed, and the *Galena* returned to service in February 1864 as an unprotected wooden gunboat. She participated in the Battle of Mobile Bay in August 1864, and ended the war as part of the Western Gulf Blockading Squadron.

INDEX

COMPANION SERIES FROM OSPREY

ESSENTIAL HISTORIES
Concise studies of the motives, methods and repercussions of human conflict, spanning history from ancient times to the present day. Each volume studies one major war or arena of war, providing an indispensable guide to the fighting itself, the people involved, and its lasting impact on the world around it.

MEN-AT-ARMS
The uniforms, equipment, insignia, history and organization of the world's military forces from earliest times to the present day. Authoritative text and full-color artwork, photographs and diagrams bring over 5000 years of history vividly to life.

ELITE
This series focuses on uniforms, equipment, insignia and unit histories in the same way as Men-at-Arms but in more extended treatments of larger subjects, also including personalities and techniques of warfare.

CAMPAIGN
Accounts of history's greatest conflicts, detailing the command strategies, tactics, movements and actions of the opposing forces throughout the crucial stages of each campaign. Full-color battle scenes, 3-dimensional 'bird's-eye views', photographs and battle maps guide the reader through each engagement from its origins to its conclusion.

ORDER OF BATTLE
The greatest battles in history, featuring unit-by-unit examinations of the troops and their movements as well as analysis of the commanders' original objectives and actual achievements. Color maps including a large fold-out base map, organisational diagrams and photographs help the reader to trace the course of the fighting in unprecedented detail.

WARRIOR
Insights into the daily lives of history's fighting men and women, past and present, detailing their motivation, training, tactics, weaponry and experiences. Meticulously researched narrative and full-color artwork, photographs, and scenes of battle and daily life provide detailed accounts of the experiences of combatants through the ages.

AIRCRAFT OF THE ACES
Portraits of the elite pilots of the 20th century's major air campaigns, including unique interviews with surviving aces. Unit listings, scale plans and full-color artwork combine with the best archival photography available to provide a detailed insight into the experience of war in the air.

COMBAT AIRCRAFT
The world's greatest military aircraft and combat units and their crews, examined in detail. Each exploration of the leading technology, men and machines of aviation history is supported by unit listings and other data, artwork, scale plans, and archival photography.

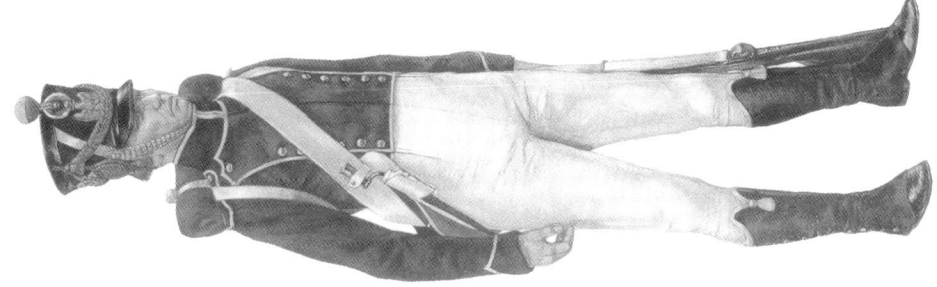

FIND OUT MORE ABOUT OSPREY

❏ Please send me a FREE trial issue
 of Osprey Military Journal

❏ Please send me the latest listing of Osprey's publications

❏ I would like to subscribe to Osprey's e-mail newsletter

Title/rank

Name

Address

Postcode/zip   state/country

e-mail

Which book did this card come from?

❏ I am interested in military history

My preferred period of military history is _____

❏ I am interested in military aviation

My preferred period of military aviation is _____

I am interested in *(please tick all that apply)*

❏ general history   ❏ militaria   ❏ model making
❏ wargaming   ❏ re-enactment

Please send to:

USA & Canada: Osprey Direct USA, c/o Motorbooks
International, P.O. Box 1, 729 Prospect Avenue, Osceola,
WI 54020

UK, Europe and rest of world:
Osprey Direct UK, P.O. Box 140, Wellingborough, Northants,
NN8 2FA, United Kingdom

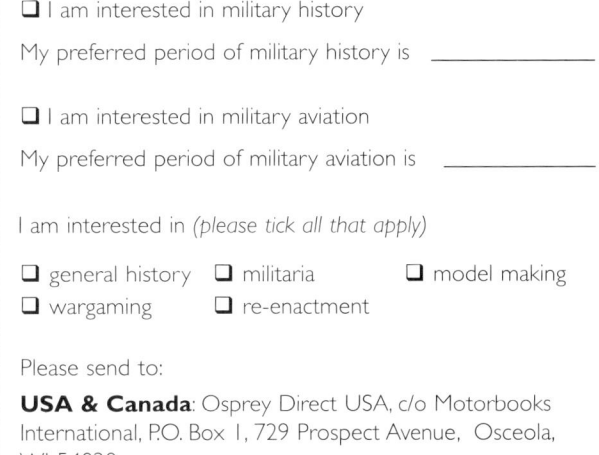
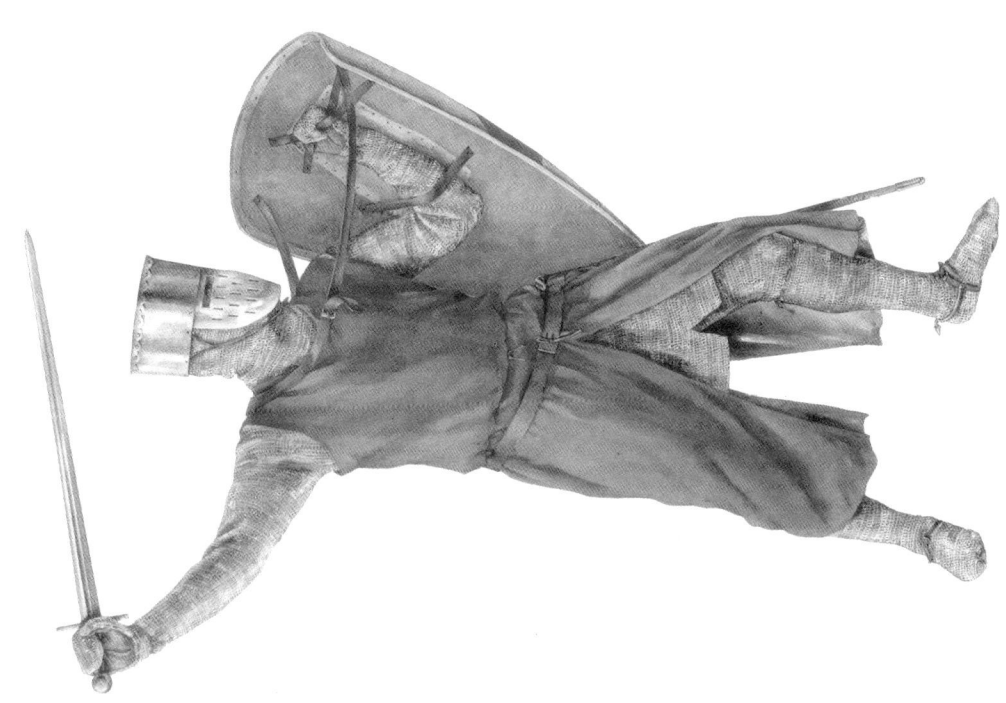

OSPREY
PUBLISHING

www.ospreypublishing.com

call our telephone hotline
for a free information pack

USA & Canada: 1-800-458-0454
UK, Europe and rest of world call:
+44 (0) 1933 443 863

Young Guardsman
Figure taken from *Warrior 22:*
Imperial Guardsman 1799–1815
Published by Osprey
Illustrated by Christa Hook

Knight, c.1190
Figure taken from *Warrior 1: Norman Knight 950 – 1204AD*
Published by Osprey
Illustrated by Christa Hook

POSTCARD